OBAMAKARMA

OBAMAKARMA

LESSONS ON LIVING
INSPIRED BY THE 44TH PRESIDENT

Russell Razzaque

FEBRUARY BOOKS

http://www.februarybooks.com

Library of Congress Cataloging-in-Publication Data

Razzaque, Russell.
Obama karma : lessons on living from the 44th president/Russell Razzaque.—1st ed.
p. com.
ISBN 978-0-9849543-1-5
Self-help. 2. Personal growth. 3. Eastern philosophy. 4. Title.
2012932306

ISBN 978-0-9849543-1-5
eISBN 978-0-9849543-3-9

Printed in the United States of America

Book design by Casey Hampton

FOR MUM, DAD AND MARIA

All my wisdom grows from the seeds of your love.

CONTENTS

OBAMAKARMA

A COURSE IN KARMA

t was an election night party in San Diego, November 4th, 2008. All manner of food and drink decorated the bar and tables in the cavernous function room, but virtually none of it had been touched for over an hour. The polls had just closed in California and all eyes were glued to the screen. The young people surrounding me seemed to collectively hold their breath in anticipation of something only six months ago they dared not dream would happen. Then it flashed onto the screen. CNN declared: "Barack Obama will be the 44th President of the United States of America." The room erupted. What seemed to be a decade of bottled-up emotion gushed out over everyone present. There were laughter and tears, clapping and hugs, high-fives and kisses. I looked out of the window and a homeless man was dancing in the street.

America had elected its first African-American President, but, having watched the campaign keenly for the past several months, I had come to learn that for many millions of people Obama's appeal ran even deeper than the revolution his ethnicity represented.

There was, I sensed, a certain quality he demonstrated through the campaign that drew support to him in a way that is uncommon in modern politics.

Knowingly or not, he seemed to touch upon it himself in his acceptance speech:

> "I was never the likeliest candidate for this office. We didn't start with much money or many endorsements. Our campaign was not hatched in the halls of Washington. It began in the backyards of Des Moines and the living rooms of Concord and the front porches of Charleston. It was built by working men and women who dug into what little savings they had to give $5 and $10 and $20 to the cause.
>
> "It grew strength from the young people who rejected the myth of their generation's apathy... who left their homes and their families for jobs that offered little pay and less sleep.
>
> "It drew strength from the not-so-young people who braved the bitter cold and scorching heat to knock on doors of perfect strangers, and from the millions of Americans who volunteered and organized."

There seemed to be an invisible attractive force bringing these people together. And, though the years since have seen a series of ups and downs in Obama's achievements and fortunes, there was always something that a significant portion of the American public recognized: a rare combination of inner peace and outer passion, reason and idealism. These qualities ensured a high level of respect and affection for him, no matter his political standings. Though I had never seen anything on this scale in my lifetime, I recognized what lay at its core.

———

In 1990, a Yale University professor worked with a colleague to scientifically identify the specific characteristics that were shared by people who were, on average, more successful in life, both personally and professionally. What they discovered was that the correlation was less related to intellectual intelligence, and more related to things like identifying our own feelings, identifying the feelings of others, and openly facing and managing emotional issues. They termed this Emotional Intelligence.

At the core of Emotional Intelligence is self-awareness: The more we are in touch with our own feelings, the more we can connect with others. And the more we connect with the feelings of others, the more we are able to cooperate and support one another, and ultimately make progress in the areas of our choice. These findings coincided with other recent discoveries in evolutionary biology. A common misconception about our evolutionary story was that success was based on "survival of the fittest." Notions such as the "selfish gene" conjured up images of a dog-eat-dog world in which only the most ruthless would survive. Modern biology has proved this perspective to be false.

The actual reason mankind evolved beyond other species was our ability to act with compassion. Compassion and cooperation resulted in better protection and preservation of our communities and enabled us to pass on knowledge so that each generation could build on the progress of the last.

Emotional Intelligence has been the invisible cornerstone of human progress. And it is recognized wherever it exists, particularly in people who possess it to a high degree.

Emotional Intelligence is Obama's dog whistle, resonating with millions of like-minded people around the world. Whether they know it or not, this is perhaps the prime quality that has drawn so many to him through thick and thin.

And you possess it too. That is why you are reading this book.

Learning from others, or *modeling*, is one of the best means of self-improvement known in psychology. This book is designed to achieve that, using the 44th President of the United States as its subject. Everyone possesses elements of Emotional Intelligence from which we all can learn, but Barack Obama makes a particularly good case study at this moment in history being (agree with him or not) one of the world's most visible people, who also happens to have a high emotional intelligence.

Obama has his flaws like anyone else, and the book will pull no punches as we openly explore those too; for just as we can learn from our own shortcomings, so we can learn from those of others. Accepting the fallibility of others *without judgment* is an important step toward accepting our own fallibility. The key is to be judgment-free at all times by recognizing that no one exists without weaknesses, pressure points and blind spots; and approaching them with understanding means we will be able to provide the same understanding to ourselves.

Ultimately, Obama's Karma is the way in which his inner world is manifested in the outer world. It's the same for all of us. The one thing—perhaps the only thing—we have control over is ourselves; but that is all we need.

By working on ourselves and transforming our inner world, we possess the ability to transform the outer world around us.

That is the objective of this book.

Throughout this book we will be exploring and improving ourselves through practical exercises. Our starting point will always be self-awareness. One of the founders of modern psychology—even if we don't follow his whole textbook of theories today—provided, for me, the best analogy for the importance of self-awareness. Freud wrote of an invisible elephant that we all travel on. At any point in time we are actually being carried through life by a force with which we are unfamiliar—our unconscious—and as a result we often face frustration, disharmony or disappointment when our needs, goals or ambitions are thwarted. In other words, half of us (the conscious half) doesn't know what the other half (the unconscious half) is doing. And, indeed, the unconscious part may be more than a half—much more. Gaining awareness of the deeper layers of our self and becoming more conscious is essential to success, peace and happiness.

An important thing to note, however, is that we will never gain full awareness of all parts of our self. Don't expect to get to a point where you know it all. Our unconscious is a metaphor for the dynamic and constantly evolving thoughts and feelings of our inner world, and so the work of self-awareness never ends. The goal of this book is to open a window that allows us to look within.

Over my years of professional and personal learning, I have discovered what I believe are effectively wormholes to the inner self. I learned the foundation of these techniques not from an esteemed colleague or revered professor, but from a young Austrian woman named Natascha Kampusch. You may remember the tragic story of a girl who was abducted in 1998 at the age of ten. The kidnapper locked her in a basement where he controlled her completely for over eight years; from rationing her food to determining when she could wash, speak, see the sky, and sleep. He physically beat her in horrific ways and sexually abused her as well. Finally, over three thousand days after her abduction, she managed to escape.

Natascha's story was covered extensively by the media at the time and she was brave enough to face the cameras and speak of her ordeal directly several times. Her bravery and resilience struck me, but I didn't know how she would fare in the outside world, or whether she might live or die.

A couple of years later another such story came to light, also in Austria, in which a man named Josef Fritzl was found to have done the same thing to his daughter, whom he kept confined in his basement with several of her children, fathered by him through his repeated rape of her. This was, of course, a tremendous shock to the world, and the first person the media went to—to understand how someone could survive such an unspeakable trauma— was Natascha Kampusch. By now she was a composed and confident woman. The difference was remarkable. They asked her, how could these poor people ever get through such a horrific nightmare as this? She paused a moment, nodded, then looked into the distance and uttered, with total serenity, a single word: "Silence," she said. "They will need a lot of silence."

A sudden realization came upon me. This woman seemed to have overcome so much; she had traveled an enormous distance in such a short space of time, and all she needed to do this was silence. People go though years of therapy after experiencing a fraction of what she did to gain some closure, yet her answer was simple. *Silence.*

It was in the stillness that she faced her pain.

As a psychiatrist, I have treated people with a variety of traumas and abuses in their past, and I have utilized a broad spectrum of techniques, including a range of therapies and medicines to help rid them of their pain. Natascha's story helped me understand that in our rush to find solutions and pathways out of our problems, the very thing we are doing —running away—might sometimes risk making it worse.

It is only when we stand still and face the reality within that we have a chance of moving forward.

The problem is that sitting with ourselves is not easy. How much time have you spent in the last month, year, or your entire lifetime, being still, present and fully in the moment? Can you even remember the last time you were completely still? That should tell you how rare and difficult it is. And the reason it is difficult is that if you are still for long enough—just a matter of minutes—you start to feel the full force of the reality and, yes, the pain contained inside you. This is not an easy landscape to sit in for any of us. In fact, we spend much of our lives trying to avoid it by constantly keeping ourselves busy. The truth is, though, that pain in life is unavoidable. The greatest irony is that the one way we can live a happier life is through an acceptance of the unavoidable pain within. Through stillness we gently sink ourselves into the uncomfortable, yet liberating, truth of our existence. But it takes time and practice.

This book is a self-improvement program, and although we are using the life of Barack Obama as an example, its ultimate aim is to reacquaint you with yourself. It is through Obama's ability to face his own pain that he has managed to grow continually throughout his life. And I hope that by the end of this book you will be better placed to do the same.

Stillness works as a route to discovering our inner selves and our inner pain because it enables us to connect with our bodies. Our bodies act like giant reservoirs of feeling, storing the gallons of emotion we accumulate during our lives. Our emotional memory sits deep inside us, dispersed throughout our bodies. We have all experienced times when we felt so distressed emotionally that it almost felt like a physical pain; that is because the place the emotional pain actually resides is in the body. This is why there is such a strong connection between our emotional state and our physical health. Only a few short decades ago, the medical profession viewed the mind and the body as two almost fully separate parts of us. But then, as medical science's understanding of causality advanced, it was found that illness after illness was, in fact, linked to stress levels and our emotional state. Now, whether high blood pressure, heart disease, stroke, cancer, bowel problems, respiratory illness, or other serious conditions, there are proven links between our emotional state and our physical health. Our body is where our emotional world sits.

Throughout the book, we will be experiencing ourselves anew by accessing the language of our bodies through a variety of exercises and meditations that I have developed over a decade of evolving professional and personal practice.

People sometimes shrink from meditation, but as you work through this book you will be introduced to it gradually along with techniques that make it enjoyable and profoundly effective. Together with other forms of mental exercise, you will find yourself gently becoming more and more comfortable with, well . . . yourself. And what could be more important than that?

As this book is laid out in the form of a self-improvement course, we will begin with an outline of the syllabus we are about to cover:

LESSON 1: BE FLEXIBLE LIKE WATER

In his first month as president, facing a furor around a third cabinet nominee whose tax returns had been called into question, Obama gave an interview in which he uttered three words never before heard from the mouth of a President: "I screwed up!" He wasted no time openly and publicly admitting that he was fallible and capable of mistakes.

Water is the most flexible of common elements, yet it is the strongest of all, capable of cutting through rock and fashioning whole landscapes. Possessing such flexibility in the psychological realm comes from the ability to ride our own inner waves of ups and downs, highs and lows. It means an ability to flow with life rather than resisting it yet, at the same time, ultimately heading in the direction we desire. Gaining an awareness of ourselves and mastering our inner world becomes the basis of a deep, inner strength, upon which we can consequently build outer stability. We develop a faith that "this too shall pass," that we can learn from the experiences and not let them stop us.

The chapter will list occasions in which Obama has utilized this flexibility to great advantage in his life, not least in plotting, and continually correcting, his course to the presidency. We will go on to explore the origin of his flexibility built, in many ways, in opposition to his own late father's apparently tragic lack of this very quality.

The end of the chapter contains a meditation to help us visualize the water-like nature of our inner world, and by mastering it, find greater happiness and purpose in the outer world, too.

LESSON 2: RELAX INTO UNCERTAINTY

The post-New Year's festive lull of January 2011 was abruptly broken by the tragic massacre in Tucson, Arizona on January 8th. What followed was an instant political firestorm that seemed to escalate by the day. The left blamed the fiery rhetoric of the right for fuelling the instability of the killer's mind when he brutally extinguished six lives, including that of a nine year old girl, Christina-Taylor Green, and critically wounded Congresswoman Gabrielle Giffords. The right then turned on the left for what some said were their own ideological associations to the confused political views of the killer. Obama's memorial speech at the end of the week served as a uniting moment for the nation. And he did it by starting with a simple point that everyone seemed to have ignored. The truth was that nobody knew or could ever claim to know the killer's motives. In our inability to understand the workings of an individual's mind, we should not inadvertently ignite the flames of conflict.

Sometimes *reality* is the hardest place to stay, because there is often so much about it we don't know. We each have a unique way of perceiving the world—often there are aspects of life that fall completely outside of our "radar." When these things pop up, we may not know how to deal with them. As a result we feel anxious and insecure. We invest a great deal of energy into avoiding uncertainties; we manufacture imagined certainties (our perception that "this is the way things are") and these tend to trip us up. The best way to keep our feet on the ground is to know that there is much we don't know—and that our perspective is but one of many. Embracing uncertainty (however unwelcoming it may be), rather than running away from it, helps us maintain our grip on reality. This always reaps dividends in the long run. Every uncertainty can, in its own way, be relished—for beneath every uncertainty lies untold possibility.

This is key to Obama's *modus operandi*, even in relation to his religious beliefs, which we will explore in this chapter too. The chapter will end with a powerful exercise that will help us conceptualize, hold and, ultimately, relish our own inner uncertainties.

LESSON 3: EMBRACE IMPERFECTION

In his Nobel Peace Prize acceptance speech Obama talked candidly about the inevitability of conflict and war in human nature. Rather than mollify his audience with a series of anti-war platitudes, he made clear that he was not a pacifist. That vision, he believed, was a utopian one. He then went on to say that the reality of conflict as part of human nature should never absolve us of the responsibility of constantly striving to avoid, reduce and cease it wherever we can.

In this speech, he revealed a fundamental psychological perspective. In order for any progress to occur, we must accept the world as it is. This becomes our starting point. Only through an acceptance of "what is" will we then be able to effect change. This fundamental tension between change and acceptance is a paradox at the heart of life and it translates to every one of us on a personal level in our everyday lives.

The chapter looks more deeply into this central tension and goes on to provide further examples in which Obama has utilized this perspective. This includes the way he handled the race issue in America when it arose in relation to the comments made by Reverend Jeremiah Wright during his election campaign, as well as in his respectful yet determined attitude toward the Muslim world and foreign policy as a whole.

We are all imperfect children of an imperfect world, but we are all also capable of limitless change. We will end with a meditation upon the diverse and imperfect nature of the Universe around us—both inside and out—and, ultimately, draw strength from it.

LESSON 4: MAKE SPACE FOR SHADOWS

The most important imperfections to embrace are our own. Obama is perhaps the only politician in modern history who has openly discussed, without reservation, his teenage indiscretions, flawed thinking and dalliance with drugs. We all have shadows, and this chapter will talk at length about the nature of all of our shadows, how they are formed and how they are an inescapable facet of our humanity. Our shadows only become truly empowered if we expend energy trying to suppress them. Being open to our own dark side is the best way to keep it from spiraling into self-destructive cycles.

Such spiraling is inevitable from time to time. Sometimes we float away from centered awareness and this is also to be accepted. Our shadow thrives by being in the dark and we allow it to govern us at those times when we don't bring awareness to it. Examples from my own life experience will further underline this point, before the chapter moves on to explore the way in which Obama has, at times, underestimated the shadow—both in himself and in others—which has led him into political difficulties, such as during the passage of healthcare legislation and in the 2010 midterm elections.

The end of the chapter will explore techniques through which we can maintain a constant awareness of our shadow.

LESSON 5: CONNECT TO A CORE

One of the most important jobs in Obama's White House is, believe it or not, the head of the mail room. Obama placed a close personal friend and senior manager from his staff in that post. Why? Because the letters he receives from the American people, hearing about their troubles and needs, is of prime importance to him. After sifting through the vast numbers with his sizeable staff, Mike Kelleher will bring Obama about ten representative letters a day, and the president will often carry these around with him and ask people, as legislation is crafted, how this or that proposal may help the individuals whose hardships he has just been reading about. For Obama, staying connected with the suffering of others is fundamental to how he does his job, and the chapter will go on to elaborate a number of examples of this compassionate focus.

Staying grounded to our compassion is a way of staying grounded to our core, because compassion is central to who we are. Recent findings in genetics and neurobiology have shown how previous theories of human evolution via a process of "survival of the fittest" are now being replaced by a more likely "survival of the kindest." It has been shown that our ability to protect, look after and nurture our own kind, and live in complex interdependent communities is what has, in fact, driven our evolution beyond that of other species.

The chapter ends with a meditative exercise that will help us better locate and connect with the compassion that is fundamental to our core.

LESSON 6: MIRROR RESPECT

Paul Tewes was a veteran Iowa Democratic organizer. He knew the state like his own family and he was used to organizing for Democratic candidates. He signed up to Obama's campaign early on as the senior organizer in the make-or-break first primary state. He was used to providing detailed run downs of his work to the candidates he campaigned for, and several weeks into the Obama campaign he was in the car briefing Obama on all the work he had done to date, when suddenly Obama stopped him mid-sentence. "You know I trust you," Obama told Tewes. "You guys know what you're doing. Keep doing what you're doing." Tewes was taken aback. His new boss really did trust him.

Respect has always been a hallmark of Obama's dealings with the people around him. If you truly respect yourself then you cannot help but disseminate this aura by treating others with respect and so expecting the best from them, too. From respect for the self flows respect for others. And the greatest way to respect someone is to trust them to be independent—to honor their capacity for autonomy. That might need time and facilitation, but it should always be the goal. That is how change is created for the better. This is an ethos, the chapter will demonstrate, that Obama has promoted throughout his presidency, particularly in the way he handles his own team. This was especially noticeable straight after winning the election when he took the entirely unpredicted step of bringing his once bitter foe Hillary Clinton into his own cabinet as Secretary of State.

Realizing the extent to which we respect others in our lives is a good indicator and reminder of the extent to which we respect ourselves too. The exercise at the end of the chapter is designed to enhance our awareness of this most important behavior.

LESSON 7: GAIN STRENGTH FROM PAIN

There are numerous examples of pain and failure throughout Obama's career—from his failure to be elected to Congress when he first attempted it over ten years ago, to the litany of contests he lost to Hillary Clinton during the grueling 2007–2008 presidential primary campaign. What sets him apart is the way in which he reacted to them. He actively sought to embrace each one and, in so doing, converted it into a fuel for his further growth. The earliest, deepest and most powerful example of this is Obama's tenuous, fractured and ultimately unfulfilled relationship with his father.

This chapter is about growing through pain and failure. In the same way that creation follows destruction in the natural world, so it is with the human psyche, too—if we pay attention to the lessons and feelings that flow from each dark moment. The chapter ends with a powerful meditative technique to help us find strength from the pains of life.

LESSON 8: STAY IN THE TENSION
(DON'T LET THE ODDS GET YOU DOWN)

In his memoir *The Audiacity to Win*, Obama's campaign manager David Plouffe entitled his second chapter, describing the launch of Obama's presidential campaign, "Taking Off While Affixing the Wings". This analogy encapsulated Obama's highly improbable movement. The state of high tension and low probability through which he drove himself from the start was a test of endurance. But he stayed with it. He has proven to be a master of staying on the edge of one's comfort zone in order to keep growing. This is a key lesson, one that is further explored in this chapter. Obama has exemplified this ethos again and again as he has taken on major tasks and causes for himself, such as the focal point of his first term: achieving near-universal healthcare for the United States.

If we really want to reach our highest potential, we need to be prepared to take on the discomfort that the unknown or the next step brings us. This will mean taking on things that are uncomfortable and also long shots, and not avoiding accepting a challenge just because of the risk of failure (however high that may be) so long as it is fundamentally consistent with our values. That's why knowing our values is an essential tool in our kit when it comes to leading a purposeful and productive life, and the exercise in this chapter will help us determine what they are and keep a light shined on them at all times.

The final meditation is designed to help us find a place of productive tension within so that, over time, we will feel the need to resist it less and instead rise to it more.

HOMEWORK

The advice in the final chapter is to look inwards, because, though we can learn so much from others, the ultimate source of wisdom is within.

This chapter puts into context some of the exercises from previous chapters, all of which center around helping us maximize our potential by living in the present. Working on our ability to be present is like working on a muscle. In the long run, it ensures we always continue to strengthen and grow. The chapter ends with some final advice about how to stay present in our daily lives—for, I have found, this is the best karma of all.

All the meditations described in the book are also available online where I narrate them personally in an audio-visual presentation for you to follow. The links are provided before each meditation, or alternatively you'll find them listed on the readers' website: http://www.obamakarma.org/reader.html

To log in you will just need to enter the password: launch.

I recommend you leave a couple of days' gap between each chapter to enable you to practice the meditation within it several times before moving onto the next.

Now, when you're ready, let's begin . . .

BE FLEXIBLE LIKE WATER.

From day one in the White House, Obama was required to captain several ships simultaneously. Healthcare reform was a signature issue that he placed at the heart of his campaign, but at the same time, he inherited an economy hurtling towards the kind of devastation unseen in over a generation. Part of the root cause of its collapse was a system of incentives and bonuses within the financial sector that had become perverse. Even after receiving bailouts from the state, several banks were still paying out six and seven-figure bonuses to top executives. Obama's aim was to steer both these ships. While recruiting an experienced staff to his healthcare team, he also began to give speeches on the economy, particularly the importance of limiting bonuses for bankers.

Within weeks of the inauguration, these two vessels started to veer towards each other. A collision looked imminent. While he spent his days lecturing bankers on the need for restraint, anomalies began to surface in the tax records of one member of his new team after another. One of the biggest problems arose with the man he had lined up to be his healthcare czar from the beginning of his campaign: Former Senator Tom Daschle. Daschle had to pay back $140,000 of unpaid taxes, and all the while Obama consistently defended him. Nevertheless, the level of concern around his nomination for such a key post in the administration began to grow. The looming nomination fight started to look like the mother of all distractions and, at the end of January, a *New York Times* editorial came out against him. On February 3rd Daschle threw in the towel. He was out.

Obama instantly realized that he had handled the situation badly. He talked it through with his staff and decided to make a statement, the likes of which had never been uttered from a president before.

David Axelrod, his chief communication strategist, booked a series of interviews with the five major U.S. television networks for the next day for his boss before heading straight to Capitol Hill to prepare lawmakers for what was to come.

The veteran anchors were rattled by the President's words.

"I screwed up."

One or two of them did a double take.

"I've got to own up to my mistake. I'm frustrated with myself, with our team. . . . I'm here on television saying I screwed up,"

And this wouldn't be the only time it happened either, he said. Unlike virtually every president before him, Obama wanted the public to understand that he was going to make mistakes, and it was through this process of trial and error, learning and growing, that he would continually perfect his presidency.

"You know, when I think about Abraham Lincoln, what I'm struck by is the fact that he constantly learned on the job. He got better. You know, he wasn't defensive. He wasn't arrogant about his tasks. He was very systematic in saying, 'I'm going to master the job, and I understand it's going to take some time.'"

Flexibility is the power to put defensiveness aside, and continually adjust and learn from our mistakes. Not just great presidents, but successful people from all walks of life, possess this ability.

The most flexible common substance we know is water. It can flow through our fingertips and trickle through the ground, yet it is water that burrs through rock, shapes entire landscapes and carves out whole canyons. The most flexible matter is also the most powerful. And so it is with us.

When we are too passionately committed to achieving something, we sometimes tense up like an iceberg inside. This frame of mind then carries through into each part of the task before us, so we start becoming inflexible—trying, ever-harder, to barge our way through it. The little details then start to loom large and, before we know it, we've lost sight of the big picture and the small stuff has taken over. Each step then requires more and more energy and, ultimately, we end up grinding to a halt.

So many dreams, ideas, goals and ambitions will never be fulfilled for this very reason—the cycle of intransigence—the inflexible, uncompromising goal-orientated nature of our human condition. It's an inevitable and often useful aspect of who we are, but it's not always the most successful.

The best way to flow with life is to meld with its fluidity. When following an objective or working towards a goal, actually look out for the icebergs ahead. These are not icebergs that lie in the path in front of you, mind, but icebergs that grow within. When you feel yourself developing an iceberg-like desire to push at something, because it's not going your way, pause. Sit with it for a while. Try and sense what it feels like within your body. As you do, you might start to realize that you are, in fact, being overly defensive or insistent on this part of the journey going exactly the way you want when, in fact, what really matters is the big picture.

There are often many paths to any goal, and even if it isn't the case in this particular instance, the only way you'll really know is by taking some time out and giving the iceberg within you some time and space. More often than not at least some of it will melt, allowing you to flow more easily towards your goal.

This fluid flexibility around the small things is what enabled Obama to achieve the big things in his life. It was, in fact, keenly on display during the biggest challenge of his life at the time when he fought his utterly improbable campaign for the White House.

———

The campaign had dragged on for over a year. Obama had won a series of primaries but Hillary Clinton still hung on relentlessly. The night of March 4th, when both Texas and Ohio went to the polls, was their chance to end the race decisively and seize the nomination. A win in either state would have sealed the deal, but as the results poured into the thick of the night it quickly became clear that they had lost both states convincingly. The grueling primary was now set to continue for several more months.

"The press waited to call it until well after it was clear to us we had been hammered," recalled David Plouffe. "When they did and Hillary emerged to give her victory speech, I wanted to throw the TV out of the hotel window."

"Our conference room was a den of gloom. Half-eaten sandwiches and soggy coffee cups were scattered across tables. We all did a lot of cursing and sighing. It didn't matter that two weeks earlier we'd had no chance to win either big state. In the intervening days, we had moved so quickly that the prize was in our sights. Now we had blown it."

Plouffe called up to his boss. "It goes on," said Obama quietly in response. "I'll see you tomorrow."

The meeting at campaign HQ for senior staff the next morning was a tense and anxious moment. How would the candidate react to such a body blow?

"Obama started the meeting with a critique of his own performance," described Plouffe. "His major point was that in the last two weeks he had not been driving towards the finish line. He wanted the race to be over more than he wanted to win it . . . We had become too predictable and stale. He felt he needed to regain the pre-Iowa mentality . . . And he needed to regain the bounce in his step, and the sense of mission that had seemed to abandon him in the last two weeks."

His opening up in this way had an instant effect on his staff, and on the rest of the meeting. "To have a boss willing not just to shoulder blame but to do so first established an indescribably healthy dynamic. It made people less defensive and more open with their own critiques, of themselves, him, and the campaign as a whole," noted Plouffe gratefully.

The team proceeded to map out a series of subtle changes in their approach and campaign style, all of which would have a major impact on their tactics through the rest of the campaign. A corner had been turned. Corrections would be made, and the trajectory restored.

None of us are immune from the shifting sands of life. We are all battered by one wave after another, for the only constant in the Universe is change. The world around us is always in a constant state of flux; night falls on one side of the planet while the sun rises on another, winter clouds sweep in on one side of the planet while the flowers of spring bloom on another, a monsoon rains on one side of the planet while a drought rises in another, peace returns to one region of the world, while war breaks out in another, and farther afield, suns burn while others collapse, galaxies collide while others re-form.

So, sitting as we do within these wider cycles, we have two choices: One is to ride the waves as they come, experiencing them one by one. The other choice is to resist them, fight against them and ultimately become overwhelmed by them. If we are to choose the former, then we must start within and become aware of how we perceive the world.

A consistent maxim in the world of psychology—and one of the first things I learned as I began my training in it—is that, it is not events that make us happy or sad, it is how we react to them. The most important terrain to pay attention to is the inner world, which in itself is a reflection of the Universe around us.

How we perceive the outer world depends on a mix of emotions that are always in play inside us, just like the waves, currents and systems that shape the surface of the ocean. At any particular time of the day or night, a part of us is happy, a part of us is sad; a part is positive, a part is negative; a part is optimistic, a part is pessimistic; a part is grateful, a part is disappointed; a part is excited, a part afraid; a part is enthused, a part resistant; a part is inflated and a part is deflated. In this way, the fluctuations in the universe around us are a reflection of the fluctuations within us, and vice versa. It's all intertwined in a kind of cooperative cosmic dance.

Riding our own inner waves of ups and downs, highs and lows is the key to riding the waves of the outer world too. Gaining an awareness of ourselves, and the way we perceive the world becomes the basis of a deep, water-like inner strength. Through awareness of this perpetual change, we will find stillness. Through awareness of perpetual turmoil, we will find peace.

A powerful way to tap into our inner fluctuations is meditation. The first meditation in this book is a gentle exercise that will be relatively easy to start. Try it for just a couple of minutes first then, over time, you will find it easier to sit with it for longer and longer periods.

Before we commence any meditation, however, I need to tackle an issue that people often perceive as the main obstacle to meditation. In fact, it is what often leads people to believe they couldn't possibly do it, or even feel afraid of it.

Buddhists speak eloquently about what they term "monkey mind." Essentially, monkey mind refers to the way the mind jumps restlessly from thought to thought the way a monkey jumps from tree to tree. Countless people around the world have found difficulty in meditating because the feeling is that in order to meditate properly, we need to stop thinking. The problem then arises in the conflict that you feel with your monkey mind because it just won't stop!

With the conflicting feelings, positions and emotions that sit within us deep down inside, it can almost feel like a cauldron in there—smoldering away like the Earth's core. Consequently it can be hard for us to sit still and be with it. That's where the natural feedback mechanism of the mind kicks in. In many respects the mind is like a cooling fan. When the pressure or heat within becomes too great, the mind starts to whir into action. When it does, it then takes us back into the past, remembering thoughts and feelings from times gone by, or into the future, contemplating it with dreams, ideas and speculations. In other words, when we try and sit with the depth of feeling within our body, the heat that we begin to become aware of triggers off our mind into the thinking process which then, like a helicopter, transports us out of the moment and into the past or the future. It does that because it is meant to. So there is nothing wrong with it. You can't stop it anymore than you can stop yourself inhaling after an exhalation, so don't try to. When we practice stillness or meditation, and your cooling fan mind kicks in, that's fine. As soon as you realize that this is what is happening—know that it's OK. Just observe it. This observation itself is part of the meditation.

Indeed, the concept of watching our thoughts is an integral part of all meditation. In each of the meditations in this book, I will guide you through a set of metaphors and images that will enable you to contextualize your thoughts within the meditation.

When I meditate at home I am very lucky in that I have my own living metaphor just outside the window, as I live by the River Thames. When I start to meditate I hear the waves swish in and out, against the river's edge. That is exactly how my thoughts move when I meditate. They float in and then they float out. As long as I let them be—don't get trapped into them and let them pass—but never resist their return either, I can carry on for a while.

And, with a bit of practice, so will you. So let's start . . .

CHANGING WORLD MEDITATION

Read these notes then close your eyes and take yourself gently through each step. Alternatively, you will find this guided meditation, for you to simultaneously listen to and practice, online at www.obamakarma.org/world.html:

- Sit or stand in a comfortable position. Keep your back straight and unsupported, so you're relaxed but upright.
- Start by taking a few deep breaths and feel your lungs fill with clean air on the in-breath, and empty completely on the out-breath.
- Gently close your eyes or, if you prefer, leave them open but focused only softly on what is before you.

- Now spend a moment listening to the sounds around you, around the room and outside it. The sound of stillness, motion, noise or what ever happens to be there.

- Now turn your focus within. Using metaphor to open a connection to your inner world, consider your inner experience as a lake. Feel the waves of this lake ripple within you. Highs and lows, dark and light, crests and troughs flow within you.
- It is the beauty and diversity of your inner world, which is itself a reflection of the world outside too.
- Waves of happiness, sadness, fear, excitement—all the emotions and thoughts within you—flow back and forth.
- Stay with it.
- Knowing that you can face the world inside you in this way, will help you better face the world outside too, and all the changes and flexibilities it demands.
- Sit with the lake for a few minutes. Just observe. And be.
- If a feeling or thought takes you away for a moment, that's OK. Let it be. Realize that you just got sucked into a wave. It happens all the time. Then step back and remember that you are the whole lake, not any one wave. Continue, from that perspective to watch all your thoughts and feelings like waves within you.

- After several minutes, gradually return to the broader awareness of the room around you; imagine its features before opening your eyes, looking around and giving yourself a few moments to reorient.

Try this whenever you have the opportunity in the day. Even if you only have 30 seconds to yourself, close your eyes, start to focus on your breaths and watch your array of thoughts and emotions flow through you . . .

Obama is often described as a highly disciplined individual, and this tends to refer to the way in which he maintains his relaxed demeanor throughout the ups and downs that face him. "No Drama Obama" was the buzzword during the campaign. To achieve this, he had to conquer his inner world first, giving space to the fluctuations that naturally flow within it. This poise was not something he was born with. Like most human traits, it is a characteristic that has been a lifetime in the making. The seeds of it can be traced back into his childhood; particularly the profound impact his father's contrasting personality had upon him.

Barack Obama, Sr. was not the flexible, self-critiquing consensus seeker that his son became. Far from it. Barack II's brief encounters with his father were, in fact, a lesson in the opposite. But it was through that contrast that he would eventually find and define himself.

After being separated from his father at only one year old, Barack II knew of him only through legend. Barack Sr.'s soaring intellect had led him to win a scholarship to Harvard. Leaving behind his wife and son, however, he was never to return, ultimately divorcing Barack II's mother—Ann Dunham—and remarrying another American woman before returning to Kenya after his studies.

Versions of his father had played like a movie before him throughout his childhood, via the stories and photos his mother and grandparents shared with him. There never seemed to be much risk of penetrating this bubble—a comfort zone he was happily settling into—until one day a letter arrived informing the family that Barack Sr. would be visiting. "Barry," as Barack II was known at the time, was ten years old by now, and the very notion shook him to his core. Indeed, the letter had taken all of them by surprise, including his grandmother (affectionately known as "Toot") who had read it out to him, as he describes in *Dreams From My Father.*

"[At the end] she carefully folded the paper and slipped it into a drawer in the kitchen. Both she and Gramps fell silent the way, I imagine, people react when a doctor tells them they have a serious but curable illness. For a moment the air was sucked out of the room and we stood, suspended, alone with our thoughts."

The anxiety extended to his mother too, but she was determined to support her son, nevertheless, as best she could:

"My mother had sensed my apprehension in the days building up to his arrival—I suppose it mirrored her own—and so, in between our efforts to prepare the apartment we had sublet for him, she would try to assure me that the reunion would go smoothly. She had maintained a correspondence with him . . . and he knew all about me"

The anguish-laden curiosity gave way to an uncertain reconciliation between father and son. He recalls the day they met vividly; watching his father eat at the dining table among all the familiar faces of his maternal family. He noticed his slim physique and observed his movements. Who was this man, his father? Christmas Eve became an informative lesson.

"I turned on the television to watch a Christmas special—*How The Grinch Stole Christmas* . . .

"'Barry, you have watched enough television tonight,' my father said. 'Go to your room and study now, and let the adults talk.'

"Toot stood up and turned off the TV. 'Why don't you turn the show on in your bedroom, Bar.'

"'No, Madelyn,' my father said, 'That's not what I mean. He has been watching that machine constantly, and now it is time for him to study.'

"'My mother tried to explain that the cartoon was a Christmas favorite, that I had been looking forward to it all week. 'It won't last long.'

"'Anna this is nonsense. If the boy has done his work for to-morrow, he can begin on his next day's assignments. Or the assignments he will have when he returns from the holidays.' He turned to me. 'I tell you, Barry, you do not work as hard as you should. Go now, before I get angry at you.'

"I went to my room and slammed the door."

His mother came to him the next day. "You shouldn't be mad at your father, Bar. He loves you very much. He's just a little stubborn sometimes."

Every child passes through stages of relationship with their parents; they start out by idolizing them then, over time, as the scales fall from their eyes, they realize that their parents are flawed creatures (just like everybody else). For young Barry this process took place in fast forward. His image of his father came crashing to the Earth with a thud during that singular encounter. The effect of his father's stubbornness on Barry—arguing with his real guardians, his mother and grandmother, as if only he knew best—must have been marked.

They shared better times after that, but his father only stayed a month in total. On their last day they laughed together, dancing to an African music recording his father had brought especially for him.

"I took my first tentative steps with my eyes closed, down, up, my arms swinging, the voices lifting. And I hear him still."

They would never see each other again after that.

The deeper truth behind his father's inner turmoil and outer intransigence only became clear to him many years later when he traveled to Kenya to meet his father's family after his death. He was looked after by, and spent most time with, his half sister Auma. They seemed to be avoiding a conversation about their shared father for the initial days. "It was as if our conversation stopped whenever we skirted over his memory."

Then one night, over tea, she began to open up and his whole story came flooding out: Upon his return from Harvard, Barack Sr. had secured a high-ranking job with an international oil firm—Shell. He was much sought-after in those days and was close with numerous senior officials and ministers in the government who would visit him regularly. He was firmly entrenched in an elite social circle across the public and private sector and he was admired for his intellect and contribution. The Vice President was a personal friend, and there was talk of his joining the government.

He was eventually recruited to the Ministry of Tourism, and marked as a rising star. On the election of a new Kenyan President—Kenyatta—however, things started to change. Kenyatta was from the largest tribe, the Kikuyus, while Barack Sr., the Vice President and his friends were from the Luo tribe. People from the Luo tribe began to complain that prime jobs were going to men from Kenyatta's own tribe and that favoritism was on the rise. The Vice President complained publicly and soon after he was placed under house arrest. Tension flared up with protests in the streets. The government launched a crackdown, schism grew and people were killed.

Still Barack Sr.'s future—with his rare intellectual gift—remained solid, so long as he avoided putting his head above the parapet on tribal divisions. But he wouldn't. His friends warned him, time and again, to restrain himself on the issue in public, but he refused to heed anyone. He remonstrated openly that people he believed to be unqualified were being promoted into key posts in the government and, as a result, he started to attract the attention and, ultimately, ire of the new President. He began to get passed over for promotion himself and then—rather than get the message—he increased the volume of his protests, belittling his senior ministers openly for being less qualified and able than him.

Kenyatta eventually had enough. He summoned Barack Sr. to his office and summarily sacked him. Not only that, but he was black listed thereafter. No ministries would give him work and foreign companies were warned not to hire him. He sunk very low very fast, finding, in the end, only a small job in the Water Department and even then on the basis of an old friend who pitied him. He began to drink and came home increasingly intoxicated. He would scold his family, ultimately causing his second American wife, Ruth, to leave him alone with Auma.

"Sometimes I would stay up half the night waiting to hear him come through the door, worrying that something terrible had happened," she told Barack II. "Then he would stagger in drunk and come into my room and wake me because he wanted company or something to eat. He would talk about how unhappy he was or how he had been betrayed. I would be so sleepy; I wouldn't understand anything he was saying. Secretly I began to wish that he would just stay out one night and never come back."

The alcohol fuelled a serious car accident. The other driver was killed and Barack Sr. took almost a year in hospital to recover. It was after his recovery that he traveled back to Hawaii to see his son Barack II. He had planned to bring him and his mother back, but the conflicts that arose in that time made it a non-starter for Ann.

Eventually, Auma left him too—she won a scholarship to a good school before traveling to Germany to further her studies. In the end, their father moved in to a hotel room where he lived mostly alone, until he died a few years later.

The young Barack II was profoundly shaken by his father's story. In one way or another, the image of his father had guided him his whole life. "It was into my father's image, the black man, son of Africa, that I'd packed all the attributes I'd sought in myself . . . [his] voice had . . . remained untainted, inspiring, rebuking, granting or withholding approval."

Now the whole edifice had collapsed in one go and he found this, at once, both liberating and frightening. He described the moment in *Dreams From My Father*:

> "What stood in the way of my succumbing to the same defeat that brought down the old man? Who would protect me from doubt or warn me against all the traps that seem laid in a black man's soul? The fantasy of my father had at least kept me from despair. Now he was dead, truly. He could no longer tell me how to live."

Though his father could no more be a perfect example—a fantasy template—for him, he could still be a lesson. The twenty-five year old Barack Obama was now left to become his own man, able to see his father, his past and his inheritance, with objectivity and fresh eyes. He was no longer chained to it, but he was ready to learn from it.

Intransigence, inflexibility, too much certainty and a lack of humility had brought "the old man" down. In the end, according to Auma, there were signs that their father recognized this himself. Ultimately it was through his daughter that he managed to pass these lessons of his life on to his son.

Through our childhoods, we all develop an inbuilt drive to want to control the environment around us. It is an inevitable part of our nature. As babies, we experience the fear brought on by dependence and do not have any sense of assurance around how we will survive from one moment to the next. This inner sense of insecurity leads to a need to gain control in the outer world. There is nothing abnormal about it.

Our parents inadvertently add to our insecurity. Because they are human too, they will sometimes over-reach with punishments, rules and boundaries. As a result, the child will sometimes be made to feel less secure in themselves. This adds another layer of tension and controlling need, which the growing child will then act out on the people around them.

Exerting your will on another person is a way of defending yourself against an inner sense of inadequacy. Again, a degree of this is inevitable in everyone for the reasons stated above. No one has a perfect sense of security and so no one is free of a controlling streak. As a result, on becoming a parent, this control drive will be passed on to the next generation; and so the cycle continues.

Again, there is nothing abnormal about it.

Sometimes, however, it does escalate to a pathological level. People with a deep sense of inner insecurity and inadequacy can go on to become extremely controlling towards other people in a variety of ways. In my own practice I have seen it manifest in a number of personalities and disorders including, for example, obsessive-compulsive disorder and also, what is known as, anankastic personality disorder. In the former, high degrees of control are exhibited in the form of rituals that the sufferer feels compelled to perform around certain times or events in the day. I have known people to wash their hands many dozens of times a day and shower and clean the house so intensively that they are literally unable to leave the house, hold down a job or sustain any kind of relationship. The rituals are a defense against the feeling of underlying helplessness that is so great they cannot face it for a moment. Anankastic personalities are lesser degrees of obsessionality, which may not involve rituals and compulsions but will involve excessive determination to follow set patterns and routines, whether at work or in the way they relate to others. This then becomes problematic when they are confronted with the inevitable need to adapt to different situations at different times and, as a result, panic, anger or even violence—to themselves or others—may ensue.

People with these types of obsessional or anankastic personalities will cling so tightly to their way of doing things that they can easily fall into a depression. I have often spent a number of months treating people for depression before we were able to get to the original problem, which was an underlying obsessionality or overwhelming perfectionism that fuelled it in the first place.

Further towards the extreme end of the scale are, of course, those with a severely damaged sense of security who resort to dangerous and violent behaviors in the fruitless hope of proving to themselves that they are in control. This is often part of the psychological cocktail of cult leaders who insist on controlling the lives and beliefs of a mass of people.

The most severe of all is the dictator who sadistically tortures his opponents to maintain his need for order and hierarchy. The deep-seated insecurity a tyrant creates in the world around him is often a mirror of what is contained within him.

Rigidity and inflexibility, then, runs through the whole human psyche in varying degrees. We all possess it, and some of us more than others. The way we achieve harmony with the world around us is the same way we achieve harmony with our own selves; namely, to come to terms with—and not attempt to escape from—our innate sense of insecurity. The desire to control is a way of escaping this pain, but our greatest healing is in allowing ourselves to just sit with it and feel it. This is where the stillness comes in.

Once we become more comfortable with facing our own pain, we will realize that we don't need to hold on to things as tightly as we thought we did. A new lightness of touch will emerge and, from it, a whole series of alternative pathways will materialize. This is flexibility through strength and also, ultimately, strength through flexibility.

And it starts by opening up to the "control center" within us all. The part of us that needs to make sure things go exactly the way we want . . .

CONTROL CENTER EXERCISE

The times when we exert our "control center" are many and varied. The more we become aware of it, the more we will be able to recognize it, and ultimately, the less it will control us (or others, for that matter). It sits within us like an iceberg. In the same way that a clump of ice can grow, gradually incorporating everything around it, so can our control center— growing every time it is exposed to the outside world. The purpose of this exercise is then to recognize it every time it reveals itself. You can do this whenever you are faced with a situation that seems to be going against you; say gridlocked traffic, or a difficult friend, customer or relative. The desire to resolve the situation by controlling it arises within you. You want to make the other person do what you want them to do, but due to social etiquette, however, we're not always able to do that. As a result we develop a knotted feeling inside.

That's your control center.

Feel it whenever a moment like this occurs. See it is a blessing that you are able to come face to face with your control center in this moment. Investigate what exactly it feels like. Words like "knot" and "iceberg" are only my words and also, they are just metaphors. No word can ever fully describe a feeling, so by sitting with it you will be able to understand the true nature of the feeling better than any description I—or subsequently you—could ever provide.

The more time you spend with your control center through moments such as this, the more you will know it. And the more you know it, the less it will control you.

When we are no longer so attached to our control center, we start to be able to channel its energy in a number of positive ways. I once spent a brief time learning the martial art of Aikido. The essence of Aikido is learning to defend yourself from an attacker by being so flexible that you are able to blend with his energy and so prevent him from hurting you with it. For example, if someone throws a punch at you, in Aikido we are taught not to resist the punch but to quickly swivel to step beside our attacker and see the motion almost from his point of view. That puts us in an excellent position from which to slightly destabilize him and guide him into a fall from his own force.

Resisting your own desire to control someone else, and melding with them instead, is a powerful self-defense technique. The attacker will always be thrown off balance when you redirect their force rather than resist it. Disabling someone in this fashion is guaranteed every time. A black belt in Aikido is able to defend himself or herself from multiple attackers with weapons, coming at him/her with full force. The end of the attack will result in each of the attackers on the floor while the aikidoist is left standing and poised ready for the next attack. Observing such tests for black belt status is truly a wonder to behold.

As I toured the world of martial arts, observing a series of different schools, I found that possessing the flexibility to meld with your opponent as much as possible while, at the same time, being ready to use limited force in a selected and precise way is a fundamental basis for pretty much all forms of martial art. It's about combining the Yin and the Yang and being flexible enough to switch from one to the other at a moment's notice.

This, I have found, is a form of flexibility and agility that all leaders need to possess in order to be effective, particularly in times of war.

Upon assuming the presidency during what had come to be known as "the war on terror," Obama knew he needed to define his own approach to combating the threat of terrorism early on. He knew, however, that this was not an issue that could be rushed. It involved analyzing the situation on the ground in detail and marrying it with an overarching philosophy about what his administration intended to achieve and how they would achieve it. A review was put in place on day one and Obama let it run a full 16 months before drawing it to a conclusion and presenting it to the world on May 26th, 2010. A 52-page document was produced and, from the beginning, it was clear that this was a very different vision from the previous administration. "The U.S. President has instead replaced it with a softer approach stressing 'new partnerships' and multilateral diplomacy," the *Daily Telegraph* reported the following morning. In his introductory speech, Obama was clear about where the heart of his new policy lay. "Our long-term security will not come from our ability to instill fear in other peoples but through our capacity to speak to their hopes . . . This is not a global war against a tactic—terrorism, or a religion—Islam."

Obama's intention was to direct the emphasis towards deeper bridge building and away from military engagement alone. He saw this as the ultimate means to defeat terrorism. Education, support and aid were key. "Our best defenses against this threat are well informed and equipped families, local communities, and institutions."

He also talked about engaging with nations such as North Korea—but "without illusion"—as isolation, he believed, would only result in continued intransigence. Indeed, engagement was a central strand that ran through the whole document and speech. It was about forging better links with all parts of the world in which threats against the US exist and also, where necessary, providing support to them too. This was a continuation of the thinking Bill Clinton had done since leaving office when he suggested that, in addition to—or even instead of—supplying arms to Pakistan during his presidency, they would have been better served by funding an education system in that country that could have prevented the mushrooming of madrasas (Islamic religion-based schools), where poor families ended up sending their children in the absence of any other available education. These ultimately became the training grounds for the future Taliban.

Many on the right attacked Obama's announcement instantly as a "therapeutic" foreign policy. They complained that they had not heard enough about Obama's willingness to utilize the nation's military might against their foes if and when that became necessary. People began to wonder if Obama was flexible enough to use the stick as well as the carrot. Was he too wedded to a solely liberal policy of engagement?

This question was tested less than two months later when in July 2010, CIA operatives drove up behind a white Suzuki in the busy Pakistani city of Peshwar and wrote down its plate number. Driving the car was Bin Laden's most trusted courier. They had being trying to trace this man for four years and now finally they had caught sight of him.

He was followed round the clock and less than a month later, he led them directly to a high-walled compound in Abbottabad. Suspicions were immediately raised back at CIA head quarters as they discovered that, despite the size of the complex, there were no telecommunications links going in or out of it whatsoever, only the occasional highly cautious visitor. All visible windows had been darkened and they even burned their trash inside the compound instead of taking it out.

CIA monitoring escalated rapidly. They purchased a property opposite and discretely observed the comings and goings. According to *The New York Times*, "Observing from behind mirrored glass, CIA officers used cameras with telephoto lenses and infrared imaging equipment to study the compound, and they used sensitive eavesdropping equipment to try to pick up voices from inside the house and to intercept cell phone calls. A satellite used radar to search for possible escape tunnels . . . the American surveillance team would see a tall man take regular walks through the compound's courtyard—they called him 'the pacer'." They gradually built up a case that "the pacer" was probably Bin Laden. But no one was sure, as no one had seen his face.

On March 14th, 2011, the CIA Director, Leon Panetta, took the evidence to the White House. They believed it was now a 60% to 80% probability that the occupant at the center of the compound was Bin Laden. On March 22nd, Obama asked for plans of action to be drawn up. Robert Gates, the Secretary of Defense, was initially skeptical about a helicopter assault. It was too risky, he thought. The other option of an aerial bombardment or, indeed, waiting longer till they had more robust proof were in con-

stant consideration as they churned over the possibilities in the weeks ahead. The ghosts of the failed operation in 1993, known as "Black Hawk Down," where two American helicopters had been shot down and several of their crew were killed in action during a similar surgical capture attempt in Somalia, were walking through the White House. "There wasn't a meeting when someone didn't mention 'Black Hawk Down'," a senior administration official said.

Underneath it all was the basic question about the President' Would he issue the command? Could he stretch to using Ame ca's stick in this way, as well as the carrot? Just how flexible his vision? Would he authorize the use of lethal force if ne sary?

A piece in the *New York Times* described the tensions moment. It was April 29th, 2011. "Around the table, the went over and over the negative scenarios. There were lo ods of silence, one aide said. And then, finally, Obama sp not going to tell you what my decision is now—I'm go back and think about it some more.' But he added, 'I' make a decision soon.'

"Sixteen hours later, he had made up his mind. E morning, four top aides were summoned to the Diplomatic Room. Before they could brief the Pr them off. 'It's a go,' he said."

SEAL Team 6 was immediately dispatche Teams of interpreters and interrogators were p they prepared to take Bin Laden alive if possible SEALs was, of course, the highest priority. If of resistance, counter attack or even suicide b probable scenario given the philosophy of B tion—lethal force would have to be used.

"It was the longest 40 minutes of my life," described Obama in later interviews, as he and his national security team listened in as 79 commandos in four helicopters descended on the compound in the dead of night on Monday, May 2nd. The rest is, of course, history. After a predictable show of resistance from several people within the compound, Bin Laden—the world's most wanted terrorist—was killed. All 79 commandos returned safely, and Bin Laden was buried the same night in accordance with Muslim ritual.

Days later, among the findings brought home from the raid in Abbottabad, were a series of elaborate plans to launch further waves of attacks on the U.S., including killing innocent civilians on its train network to mark, in all likelihood, the tenth anniversary of 9/11 in less than five months. "He wasn't just a figurehead," said one official. "He continued to plot and plan, to come up with ideas about targets and to communicate those ideas to other senior Qaeda leaders." The *London Times* reported, "They have found in the haul, described as an intelligence mother load, that far from satisfying Bin Laden's obsessive anti-Americanism, the 9/11 attacks left him more determined to strike again at 'the Great Satan' and kill, not hundreds more Americans, but thousands."

The American public learned something new about their resident that week. In war, as well as in peace, he would not be oxed in by an inflexible philosophy. Yes, he was determined to ach out, show respect, offer support and utilize America's soft wer wherever possible, but if rapid and decisive force was ded in order to protect the innocent, then he would not shirk m doing that either. He was a pragmatist, not an ideologue. common thread throughout was a willingness to be flexible: situation would be judged on its merits and the calls made dingly.

RELAX INTO UNCERTAINTY

O bama had been President for less than six months, yet already he was embroiled in a religious controversy. Websites had been created and petitions collected in opposition to a decision he had made—considered "deplorable" by thousands. The story stirred its way up to the top of the news headlines as the anger it generated seemed to feed off itself, escalating exponentially by the day. His alleged offense related neither to decisions of war and peace, nor to the economy or healthcare, or indeed any of the pressing issues facing the country at the time. It was, in fact, all about his acceptance of an invitation to travel to Indiana and give the commencement speech at The University of Notre Dame, an institution with strong ties to the Catholic Church.

Leading the attack on the invitation was the Cardinal Newman Society, dedicated to promoting orthodoxy on Catholic campuses. The Society called the invitation a "travesty," launched an online campaign and started to gather signatures on a protest petition. 13,000 signed in less than a week. The petition read:

"It is an outrage and a scandal that 'Our Lady's University,' one of the premier Catholic universities in the United States, would bestow such an honor on President Obama given his clear support for policies and laws that directly contradict fundamental Catholic teachings on life and marriage."

Bishop John D'Arcy of South Bend, whose diocese includes Notre Dame, said he would not attend the commencement because it proposed to offer an honorary degree to President Obama, the graduation speaker. D'Arcy called for the university to "recommit itself to the primacy of truth over prestige."

Obama accepted the invitation—as had a line of presidents before him—but for the protesters, the very notion of giving a platform to someone they disagreed with in this way was unthinkable. As the event approached, despite the robust defense of Obama's invitation by the university authorities themselves, the level of anger and defiance within the more conservative elements of the Catholic community seemed to escalate through the roof. As far as they were concerned, Obama's very presence in their midst was a threat to their tightly held belief system.

Ralph McInerny, a philosophy professor at Notre Dame for more than 50 years, described the invitation as a "deliberate thumbing of the collective nose" at the Roman Catholic Church. He went on to say, "By inviting Barack Obama to be the 2009 commencement speaker, Notre Dame has forfeited its right to call itself a Catholic university,"

Ultimately 65,000 people signed the petition against Obama's attendance and on the day of the speech, several hundred anti-abortion demonstrators gathered to protest outside the school's front gate. Twenty-seven were arrested for trespassing.

Bishop D'Arcy joined a group of protesting students himself on the school's south quadrangle. He attended a prayer vigil the night before and declined to attend the commencement, instead speaking to the students who had gathered:

> "It's certainly the place for the bishop to be here. There's no doubt about that," D'Arcy told the crowd. "All of you here today are heroes, and I'm proud to stand with you."

Obama arrived knowing that he had an uphill struggle before him. He was still an unknown quantity to many in the country, and certainly to most in the hall that day: A new president, only a few months into office, and virtually unheard of in the nation only four years before that. He began in a spirit of openness, depicting his own spiritual path in his life thus far.

"I was not raised in a particularly religious household, but my mother instilled in me a sense of service and empathy that eventually led me to become a community organizer after I graduated college. A group of Catholic churches in Chicago helped fund an organization known as the Developing Communities Project, and we worked to lift up South Side neighborhoods that had been devastated when the local steel plant closed.

"It was quite an eclectic crew. Catholic and Protestant churches. Jewish and African-American organizers. Working-class black and white and Hispanic residents. All of us with different experiences. All of us with different beliefs. But all of us learned to work side by side because all of us saw in these neighborhoods other human beings who needed our help—to find jobs and improve schools. We were bound together in the service of others.

"And something else happened during the time I spent in those neighborhoods. Perhaps because the church folks I worked with were so welcoming and understanding; perhaps because they invited me to their services and sang with me from their hymnals; perhaps because I witnessed all of the good works their faith inspired them to perform, I found myself drawn—not just to work with the church, but to be in the church. It was through this service that I was brought to Christ.

"At the time, Cardinal Joseph Bernardin was the Archbishop of Chicago. For those of you too young to have known him, he was a kind and good and wise man. A saintly man. I can still remember him speaking at one of the first organizing meetings I attended on the South Side. He stood as both a lighthouse and a crossroads—unafraid to speak his mind on moral issues ranging from poverty, AIDS, and abortion to the death penalty and nuclear war. And yet, he was congenial and gentle in his persuasion, always trying to bring people together, always trying to find common ground. Just before he died, a reporter asked Cardinal Bernardin about this approach to his ministry. And he said, 'You can't really get on with preaching the Gospel until you've touched minds and hearts.'"

Obama went on to lay out what he considered a key aspect of religious belief, one that would enable people of different faiths and none to work together, just as he had witnessed in Chicago where he first found his:

"The ultimate irony of faith is that it necessarily admits doubt. It is the belief in things not seen. It is beyond our capacity as human beings to know with certainty what God has planned for us or what He asks of us, and those of us who believe must trust that His wisdom is greater than our own.

"This doubt should not push us away from our faith. But it should humble us. It should temper our passions, and cause us to be wary of self-righteousness. It should compel us to remain open, and curious, and eager to continue the moral and spiritual debate that began for so many of you within the walls of Notre Dame. And within our vast democracy, this

doubt should remind us to persuade through reason, through
an appeal whenever we can to universal rather than parochial
principles, and most of all through an abiding example of
good works, charity, kindness, and service that moves hearts
and minds."

The acceptance of doubt and the embrace of uncertainty; it
was this fundamental principle that had the power to bring people together and so facilitate cooperation, compassion, charity and
service to others. That, in the end, was the ultimate dividing line
between the speaker and those attending the commencement—
listening to, learning from and applauding each other—inside the
hall, and those protesting outside it.

———

Possessing some degree of certainty around aspects of our life is
important, but like every other comforting or pleasurable com-
modity, too much of it can become dangerous. Holding on too
tightly to too many certainties is often a reflection of a deeper
doubt that we are repressing and dare not allow ourselves to acknowledge. To some extent, this is also human. There is always
far more in the world we do not and cannot know; more, at any
one time, than we are ever prepared to admit to ourselves. Much
of our lives are dependent on trusting others who we do not
know—often people we have never met. Just driving down the
street, for example, requires us to trust the person driving in the
opposite direction. Shops run on the basis that they trust most of
their customers to pay for their goods before walking out the
door, and most of us go to sleep at night trusting the banks, and
all their employees, to keep our money safe. We also trust that
natural disasters aren't about to hit us or anyone we know.

These are all assumptions. Though they are usually safe, they are never certain. And there are many more that we rely on every day. The degree of uncertainty upon which our life rests is vast. It is like a hidden reservoir of doubt and fear that we all sit on.

Reality is a difficult place to be. As a result, we often create all manner of devices to help us avoid it. This can include anything from conspiracy theories to gut prejudices to complex belief systems—all to try and create some kind of order that can help us feel safe. Now, there is, of course, nothing wrong with this *per se*. We all need to engage in a degree of this just to survive. And, given that no one has the ability to know the whole of reality in its complete form, who is to say whose theory or belief system is more valid than anyone else's? The problem arises, however, when we start to insist on imposing our own version of reality upon others. That is when our compensation becomes overcompensation, and this is what sometimes creates the zealot. Humility then starts to disintegrate and this, in turn, is replaced by a sense of superiority and prejudice or judgment towards others.

So the very belief system that can give us comfort and purpose as we face the challenges of life—like a philosophical or political ideology or a religious belief, for example—can, if taken too far, start to become harmful to us and to the people around us. This is why touching base with the reservoir of uncertainty and anxiety that sits within us is often beneficial. It makes us more humble and also, consequently, more successful. We will be less prone to being blinkered by our preconceived notions of reality and so always open to continual adjustment and growth in what ever we do.

The cherishing of this layer of uncertainty is laced fundamentally into Obama's view of himself and his relationship with the world, and it is evidently a determining factor in his own personal religious beliefs too. It influences his choices and thinking as President and particularly comes into view when crises emerge.

———

It was a Saturday morning much like any other. Representative Gabrielle Giffords stood outside a supermarket in Tucson, Arizona with her staff and constituents to discuss the issues of the day in what had come to be known as a "Congress on Your Corner" meeting. It was one of a series of regular events she carried out, like several of her colleagues, to maintain the bond between the federal legislature and the people, and a number of residents turned up to say hello to greet their Representative and hear what she had to say. Among them was Judge John Roll. He was recommended for the federal bench by John McCain twenty years ago, appointed by President George H.W. Bush, and rose to become Arizona's chief federal judge. He was joined by Phyllis Schneck, who retired to Tucson to spend time with her seven grandchildren, as well as Dorwan and Mavy Stoddard, who grew up together in Tucson over seventy years ago, George and Dorothy Morris, and an enthusiastic nine-year-old girl named Christina-Taylor Green who wanted to learn about Congress and had visions of maybe entering politics herself one day.

Giffords arrived at 10 AM with her longstanding and dedicated outreach director, Gabe Zimmerman, and stood by a table set up for her outside the entrance to the store, saying hello to everyone there. As she chatted, a young man, Jared Loughner, walked straight up to her and fired several shots. One killed Judge Roll instantly, and one hit Giffords point-blank in the head. Loughner then turned and pointed the gun down the line. George Morris, a former Marine, instinctively tried to shield his wife, Dorothy. Both were shot. Dot passed away. Loughner carried on firing, hitting and killing Gabe Zimmerman, Dorwan Stoddard, Phyllis Schneck, and then he turned to Christina-Taylor Green. He shot and killed her, apparently without hesitation. Thirteen others were wounded during the spree and more would have died were it not for a petite 61 year-old, Patricia Maisch, who wrestled away the killer's ammunition as he was trying to reload, giving two others their chance to pounce. They managed to successfully subdue him until the police arrived.

Representative Giffords only survived because of Daniel Hernandez, a volunteer in her office, who ran through the chaos to minister to his boss, tending to her wounds to keep her alive.

It was a mass murder that shook America. The image of the beautiful nine-year-old girl, Christina-Taylor, gripped the public's imagination. She was born on September 11th, 2001. With the idealism that brought her to that event—to meet her Congresswoman and learn about government service—she personified the hope for a better future that knit the country together after that day; a hope that once again felt cruelly threatened.

Journalists began to piece together the possible mindset of the killer, given the original target of the murders—Democratic Representative Giffords. CNN started to spotlight politicians on the right, like Sarah Palin who had urged her supporters to "reload" utilizing a map containing several congressional districts—including Representative Giffords'—with the crosshairs of a gun over each one to emphasize the point. Commentators on the left ran with it, coming out in support of this rapidly evolving narrative, including a piece by Paul Krugman of the New York Times: "We don't have proof yet that this was political, but the odds are that it was . . . it's long past time for the GOP's leaders to take a stand against the hate-mongers."

The liberal blogosphere took it one step further. Markos Moulitsas, founder of the popular progressive blog *Daily Kos*, wrote

"Mission Accomplished, Sarah Palin" and Jane Fonda tweeted "Glen (sic) Beck guilty too." By the evening, MSNBC's Keith Olbermann blamed Palin, Beck and others, for inciting violence against the government—and demanded apologies from each of them.

The response from the right, however, was no less fulminating. Rightwing radio host Rush Limbaugh accused the left of using the murders to further their political agenda to allegedly bring regulation and censorship to the press. "I wouldn't be surprised if somebody in the Obama administration or some FCC bureaucrat or some Democrat congressman has it already written up such legislation, sitting in a desk drawer somewhere just waiting for the right event for a clampdown," he insisted.

Later he went even further, suggesting that the Democratic Party was attempting to help the murderer. "What Mr. Loughner knows is that he has the full support of a major political party in this country. He's sitting there in jail. He knows what's going on, he knows that . . . the Democrat party is attempting to find anybody but him to blame . . . he's got a political party doing everything it can . . . to make sure he's not convicted of murder."

Sarah Palin then moved to underscore the right's response by declaring, in a broadcast on social media, that journalists and the left had "manufactured a blood libel" against her and her colleagues. The term "blood libel" has historically been used to refer to the false claim that Jews used the blood of Christian children for their rituals.

Soon after the shootings, a new round of information that provided a further inkling into Loughner's possible motivations came to light. A former classmate described him as "quite liberal" and, apparently, his ravings included expressions of admiration for the *Communist Manifesto*. The right then seized on this, suggesting that Loughner was plainly pursuing a leftwing agenda and that those on the left, with their own fiery rhetoric, were to blame for the mass killings.

As the day of the special memorial for those who were lost approached, the atmosphere of escalating hysteria appeared to be enveloping the media and much of the country with it. Obama's address was billed as a seminal moment in his presidency. On such occasions the nation looks to the president for healing. His team knew it would be an important speech—in the same way that Clinton's reaction to the Oklahoma City bombings served as a near defining moment in his presidency at the time.

Questions abounded: How would Obama couch his contribution? Would his approach validate the left's argument or the right's? By the time of the service, however, he had made a conscious choice. He would side with neither the certainties of the left, nor the certainties of the right. He believed the lesson to be learned from this tragedy was a different one entirely.

"You see, when a tragedy like this strikes, it is part of our nature to demand explanations—to try to impose some order on the chaos, and make sense out of that which seems senseless . . . But at a time when our discourse has become so sharply polarized—at a time when we are far too eager to lay the blame for all that ails the world at the feet of those who think differently than we do—it's important for us to pause for a moment and make sure that we are talking with each other in a way that heals, not a way that wounds.

"Scripture tells us that there is evil in the world, and that terrible things happen for reasons that defy human understanding. In the words of Job, 'when I looked for light, then came darkness.' Bad things happen, and we must guard against simple explanations in the aftermath.

"For the truth is that none of us can know exactly what triggered this vicious attack. None of us can know with any certainty what might have stopped those shots from being fired, or what thoughts lurked in the inner recesses of a violent man's mind . . .

"So yes, we must examine all the facts behind this tragedy . . . but what we can't do is use this tragedy as one more occasion to turn on one another. As we discuss these issues, let each of us do so with a good dose of humility"

He resisted the temptation to use this as an opportunity to attack his political opponents. In his view, the escalating acrimony of recent days served as an object lesson in the dangers of rapidly clutching to certainties when none existed. Instead of cheering for his own side, Obama asked people to pause for a moment and sit with the uncertainty—to put temperance above vengeance and humility above certainty.

———

Our early years after high school are always a time when we are seeking to define ourselves and our relationship with the world around us. My own first days in college were a genuine revelation in this respect. Having been brought up in a relatively conservative Muslim household in the north of England, I faced a genuine culture shock when I first arrived at medical school in the vast city of London. The social life on offer to students was almost mutually exclusive to my upbringing; based, as it was, around pubs, clubs and other alcohol-based pursuits. Those of us from similar backgrounds began to cling together, as much through disorientation and even a little fear, as anything else. None of us had ever danced in a club before or drunk any alcohol, let alone gone on dates with girls. While our peers dived into the social set like fish into water, we were frantically trying to find our way through the cacophony before us. Whether it was the toga and tequila parties for freshmen, or cheese and wine with the Dean, it all seemed dreadfully foreboding to us.

Then came the freshmen's fair when the various clubs and so-
cieties of the college laid out tables for us to inspect and maybe
join if we were so inclined. At the far end of the hall I suddenly
noticed a throng of young south Asians. This looked more like
my crowd. They dressed and spoke like me, in jeans and with
goatee beards. They were a jolly crowd too, cracking jokes and
handing out delicious food; kebabs and samosas that I was miss-
ing so much since I left home. My new friends and I were eager to
learn what this club was all about and it came as somewhat of a
surprise to hear that this was, in fact, the Islamic Society.

Apart from a little Arabic on one of the posters, there was little
Islamic-looking about it. Not Islam as we had known it from our
parents anyway. Nevertheless, they seemed a fairly hip crowd, and
lured by the promise of some more nice food and much needed
companionship we decided to accept an invitation to a meeting
later that week.

The couple of meetings I attended were a revelation that has
stayed with me for the rest of my life.

My parents had always taught me the importance of respecting all people, regardless of their faith. Though they followed
their own Islamic traditions—prayed five times a day, fasted, and
remembered Allah whenever the opportunity arose—they never
considered themselves above anyone of different faiths or none.
Each person simply had their own path and this was theirs. The
Islamic Society, however, took a hammer to that perspective.

We were different from everyone else on campus, they told us.
That was a proposition none of us could deny. This, they said, was
because we were not inferior to the others around us but members
of a superior community—though a downtrodden one. They likened our plight to that of downtrodden Muslims around the
world from Bosnia to Pakistan and, as such, our loyalties were
owed to our global community. Our mission was to support and

defend them against the unbelievers. The world was divided into black and white: Those who shared our faith and those against us.

In the next meeting they built on this foundation. It was one of absolute certainty. We had a mission to redress the imbalance between our people and the unbeliever. The unbeliever was now given a name—*kufr*—a derogatory piece of slang, considered below an animal. They spoke of the need to organize and activate our brotherhood against the *kufr*. Some, I could clearly see, were gaining a newfound comfort from this new paradigm of certainty and superiority. I, however, was overcome with an increasing sense of unease.

I stopped attending the meetings, but my (now former) friends kept trying to engage me. It got to the point when I had to hide in my own house when they came to the door to stop them pestering me.

I never looked back on the experience after I left that crowd. I found my own path, integrating with an eclectic circle of friends, from all backgrounds and cultures.

Until one September day in 2001.

Reading an article shortly after 9/11, I learned of the way in which extreme Islamist recruiters would work the Universities of Europe in an attempt to draw people onto the conveyor belt of terror. The ideologies they described were identical to those I had chillingly heard in my late teens. With my own professional expertise I began to research the phenomenon and ended up putting my thoughts into a book on the psychology of suicide bombing. Key to the pathway I had discovered was a foundation of such absolute certainty that not a single inch of space for doubt was allowed.

Through my research I learned that the reason for this was due, in fact, to an inner doubt that these individuals actually possessed about themselves; their capabilities their place in the world, and their very identities. This almost existential self-doubt was nearly overwhelming. As a result, they found comfort in clinging to a creed of such absolute certainty (and superiority) that it promised to take all their fear away. It was, in fact, a poison disguised as a cure. One that, if taken to its ultimate extreme, would kill them and tens, hundreds, or even thousands of others too.

My lessons in the dangers of unequivocal, unbending certainty began early.

The fear of facing the uncertainty upon which we all sit can be so powerful that it can drive us to the most awful ends. I have come to realize that the importance of finding space in our lives and to do what seems paradoxical—relax into uncertainty—at least to a degree, cannot be overestimated. Furthermore, if appreciated for what it is, and not shunned, each wave of uncertainty can, in its own way, be converted into a form of positive energy. For ultimately, what is uncertainty if not the presence of possibility—multiple, often unforeseen, possibilities?

Through respecting and relaxing into our uncertainty, then, we can ultimately tap into a potential; a potential that always exists within us, and a potential that is virtually limitless.

Let's try it now . . .

RIVER OF UNCERTAINTY EXERCISE

There is usually a whole range of things ahead of us that cause us to experience some uncertainty—whether it's an important meeting, an interview, or even a party or a social event. There are always numerous ways these events can unfold. We usually try to ensure that we keep our anxiety over this uncertainty well hidden, but in this exercise, we are going to tap into it.

Just picture one such event in your mind's eye and then feel the currents that flow from it inside you. This is your "river of uncertainty." You have tapped into it via the uncertainty surrounding a single issue or event, but know that it is a whole river; it goes deeper and wider covering many things in your life.

Close your eyes and take some deep breaths as you feel its various currents flow within you. Allow yourself to explore this feeling for a moment—knowing, all the while, that it is perfectly natural to feel what you are feeling. Everybody does, whether they know it or not. You can fight against the current and create turbulence, or you can relax into the current and experience life as it really is.

After experiencing it for a few moments, recognize that this is your lifeblood. In the same way a river can make the land around it fertile, so can this energy you are feeling be the life force for many new and exciting possibilities in your life.

Sit with it for a few moments, and then thank the river for being there.

If you practice this regularly—befriending your fears in this way—you will find that, after a while, the currents start to calm, bit by bit.

People in senior positions in any industry are often faced with the need to make tough calls on issues where they cannot possibly know all the possible outcomes. Despite this uncertainty a choice must be made, yet it is through respecting that uncertainty—giving it time and space—that a sound decision is often reached.

When we are forced to choose between a couple of difficult options, it is often tempting to rationalize and pretend that there is less uncertainty out there than there really is. For the sake of our own comfort levels we fool ourselves into believing that one option is clearly more obvious than another. Deluding our way out of the uncertainty in order to make a decision easier is rarely a problem free way to go about things, and often it makes the situation worse in the long run than it was in the first place. Remaining true, and giving air to the fact that it is a tough call and we can never be sure about the outcome, will always strengthen our ability to face the unpredictability of the future.

George W. Bush, Obama's predecessor, had a tendency towards snap decision making—based less on the realities before him than on his "gut" which convinced him things were more predictable than they really were. Before proclaiming any judgment on the man, however, I have to say that this is a very human trait and common, to some degree, in all of us.

The contrast between these decision-making styles became most evident at exactly the moment Obama—and, indeed, the rest of the world—least expected it. In early 2011, after capping off a successful session of Congress the year before, in which a new anti-nuclear proliferation treaty with the Russians—START—was ratified by the Senate and the "don't ask, don't tell" policy that effectively prevented openly gay men and women from serving in the military, was repealed, Obama's poll numbers started to trend up again. A highly acclaimed State of The Union speech in January set a new tone and became the icing on the cake. It allowed his Senior Advisor, David Axelrod, to take his long-planned leave from the White House and enjoy a break before joining the re-election campaign the following year. Axelrod told *Politico* as he left that he finally saw a "clear field" for Obama to focus on his key message as he headed towards the general election.

He couldn't have been more wrong.

In the following months a whole region of the world seemed to turn on its head. It all started with a lone market stall owner in Tunisia.

Mohamed Bouazizi was a graduate in Tunisia who had failed to find employment in his country's poor, corruption-riddled economy. He was trying to make a meager living by selling items out of a wheelbarrow in the local market but, after failing to bribe local officials and security services, the police began threatening him with eviction from the market. On the evening of December 16, 2010, he apparently ran up approximately $200 in debt to buy the produce he planned to sell in the market the following day. His family depended on it. On December 17, he started his workday at 8 AM. Later that morning, the police began harassing him again and this time he was slapped and abused before his wheelbarrow, with all its produce, was confiscated. Bouazizi went to the local Governor to complain about this humiliation but his office refused to see him. At 11:30 AM local time he doused himself in gasoline in front of a local government building. He had experienced one humiliation after another and this time he could take it no more. He set himself on fire in public.

An entire nation—creaking under a corrupt machinery of state—sympathized with the man's plight and came out in hundreds of thousands onto the streets. Bouazizi died shortly afterwards but he had triggered a giant chain of dominoes. Within days a relentless sequence of protests and strikes forced the President of Tunisia, Zine El Abidine Ben Ali, to resign. He fled the country only to watch the revolutionary fervor spread like wildfire across the entire Middle East. One dictator after another started to take evasive measures as the long suppressed people of the Middle East rose up, almost as one.

The effects were felt in Yemen, Bahrain, Egypt, and even Iran and Saudi Arabia. After thirty years in power, Hosni Mubarak, the Egyptian President, could hold off his own country's protests no more. His undemocratic ways had finally taken their toll on the people of Egypt and, after a couple of weeks of mass protest in Tahrir Square, on February 11th, 2011, he too was forced to resign. The geopolitical framework across the whole region seemed to be redrawing itself by the day.

The Obama administration was finding it visibly difficult to keep abreast of this rapidly changing terrain. There was no doubt, though, that ultimately Obama would come out in favor of the pro-democracy movements, particularly given his own now almost prophetic speech delivered during his earlier trip to Cairo; "I want to particularly say this to young people of every faith, in every country—you, more than anyone, have the ability to remake this world . . . We have the power to make the world we seek, but only if we have the courage to make a new beginning."

Though the pace was bewildering, the choices for Western governments seemed fairly straightforward. Democratic forces would be supported wherever they were, but the local people had to take the lead. There would be no imposition of freedom at the barrel of a gun.

But then the wave hit Libya.

Colonel Gadhafi had ruthlessly suppressed his people and held power for over forty years. In that time he sponsored naked acts of terrorism abroad such as the Lockerbie bombing, and, through his multilayered secret police and security services, brutally quashed any flicker of opposition at home. Nevertheless, his relationship with the West had undergone somewhat of a rapprochement in recent years, particularly after an embrace by the former UK Prime Minister Tony Blair during the Iraq War. The evidently cordial atmosphere between the two men began to cas-

cade across the international community, gradually bringing
Gadhafi's regime in from the cold.

But no more. Emboldened by their fellow Arabs, the people of
Libya refused to obey the regime any further. Protests in the
streets turned to open rebellion and soon enough, the rebels
started taking one city after another. The world marveled at their
bravery as young men and women defied the regime, openly pro-
fessing their willingness to die for freedom from dictatorship.
Gadhafi became almost isolated in his capital, and many believed
the end was near. William Hague, the British Foreign Secretary,
started spreading rumors that Gadhafi had boarded a plane and
was en route to Venezuela.

Only no one had told Gadhafi that.

Gadhafi had maintained an iron grip on Libya for decades
and he wasn't about to give up without a fight. As his son, Saif
al-Islam, put it, "We have three plans. Plan A; we live and die in
Libya. Plan B: we live and die in Libya. Plan C: we live and die in
Libya!"

While doctors, lawyers and a portion of educated society
started to organize their own government in parts of the country,
Gadhafi launched his counter attack. Whole towns were shelled
and before long he started to launch bombing raids from the air
against his own people. Over a hundred thousand Libyans fled to
Egypt. Gadhafi railed against those revolting against him, referring to them as "drug addled cockroaches." A major offensive was
then planned as Gadhafi prepared to decimate the cities held by
the rebels. He vowed to destroy every one of them "house by
house!"

All eyes turned to the US for leadership to help the cause of
freedom in Libya. On March 3, President Obama announced that
Gadhafi "must go." A no-fly zone was suggested as a way the
West could help; at least it would prevent Gadhafi from attacking

his people by air. The drumbeat for aerial action started to grow across the international community. Even the usually inactive Arab League announced its support for a no-fly zone over Libya.

Despite the desire to help the people of Libya, however, no one knew for sure what the effect of a no-fly zone—or any military action for that matter—would actually be or where it might lead. Obama took a moment to pause and began to explore the options before the international community.

Other world leaders, however, grew quickly impatient. They pushed for an immediate UN resolution authorizing the no-fly zone idea.

The political editor of the BBC, Nick Robinson, described the tensions emerging: "London and Paris have made their move without knowing whether the United States will back it. The question that is ringing around Downing Street is 'what on earth does Obama think?' . . . David Cameron is trying hard to hide his frustration with President Obama. I'm told that he's not always succeeding."

Obama, however, was busy assessing the extent of the unintended consequences such a campaign might unleash. Who were they dealing with on the anti-Gadhafi side? What kind of regime might follow after the fall of such a ubiquitous state apparatus as Gadhafi's? Would it be a civil war? How much more deeply might the US get dragged in? Would attacking yet another Muslim country further alienate the Muslim community and so risk America's security in the long run? And what if he wasn't deposed quickly? Would Gadhafi himself resort to his tried-and-tested terrorist ways in retaliation? The uncertainty needed to be embraced. This was not a decision to be taken lightly.

The list of international politicians exuding visible frustration with Obama, however, grew by the day. The French Foreign Minister asked the French Assembly rhetorically, "what of American power?" The BBC's Mark Mardell put the scene into a broader perspective: "Many in Britain and the rest of Europe cheered when Obama was elected, and they were fed up with the guy in the cowboy boots who shot from the hip. They seemed pleased that the USA had a President with no aspiration to be the world's sheriff. Now some are shaking their heads, looking for a leader."

Having tabled a motion for a no-fly zone in the UN, Britain and France awaited word from Washington. Gadhafi then upped the ante. His troops had fought their way to the outskirts of the most populous city that opposed him, Benghazi. Virtually the whole city was his declared enemy, and he wasn't going to let them go. He was preparing to crush an entire metropolis. Genocide was imminent.

It was at that moment that Obama moved to act. He dispatched his UN Ambassador, Susan Rice, with a simple message for the assembly; a no-fly zone wouldn't be enough. More was needed. Obama wanted broader authority for military action—everything short of an invasion.

The contrast in the nature, value and style of his decision making, compared to his contemporaries on the world stage was described in a piece for *The Huffington Post* by Christina Patterson—writer and columnist for *The Independent*—posted on March 26th, 2011:

"Obama, like every other person on the face of this planet, doesn't know if bombing certain targets in Tripoli, and Benghazi, and Misrata, is going to get rid of Muammar Gadhafi , or if it's just going to strengthen his resolve. He doesn't know if the bombs will just destroy machinery, and kill soldiers, or if they're going to kill men and women who are used as human shields. He doesn't know if the so-called rebels, who

said they didn't want international help, and then that they
did, but might change their minds again, and who are mostly
about as experienced in using AK-47s and rocket-propelled
grenades as I am, will be able to stand up against a trained
army, and highly paid mercenaries, and massive supplies of
arms that the West sold them, and now wishes it hadn't. He
doesn't know if this is the kind of military action that can be
done quite quickly and cleanly, or if, like most military action, and even military action that looks as though it can be
done quickly and cleanly, it can't.

"It is, presumably, because he doesn't know these things
that he took a while to weigh them up. He may have thought,
like David Cameron, that a 'no-fly zone' sounded like a good
idea, but he probably also thought you didn't get one just by
telling the people who would have flown there that they
shouldn't. He may have thought that what you had to do to
stop people flying there may have been too risky, or too complicated, or too likely to lead to things you couldn't control, to
be worth doing. This may be why, when he said he had decided to take action to impose one, he didn't sound like a hero
who was going to save people from a terrible situation, and
who expected a round of applause. He sounded like a man
who had had to make a very, very difficult decision. And who
knew that you couldn't know whether some decisions were
right or wrong, but that you just had to live with the consequences of the one you'd made."

Resolution 1973, authorizing "all necessary measures" to protect the civilians of Libya passed the UN Security Council the
next day with ten votes for and none against. Within 72 hours of
passing the resolution, cruise missiles were launched from US
ships and an international force began bombing Gadhafi's mili-

tary. Within a week they started to withdraw. Benghazi had literally been saved by the action and genocide averted.

It could all have been very different. Tom Malinowski described, in an article for *The New Republic* on March 27th, what
might have happened had action not been taken. "Precisely because the international community acted in time—before Qaddafi retook Benghazi—we never saw what might have happened
had they not acted. Today in eastern Libya, there are no columns
of refugees marching home to reclaim their lives; no mass graves
testifying to the gravity of the crisis; no moment that symbolizes a
passing from hope to horror. The sacking of Benghazi was the
proverbial dog that didn't bark . . . But before the debate moves
on, as it must, we should acknowledge what could be happening
in eastern Libya right now had Qaddafi's forces continued their
march. The dozens of burned out tanks, rocket launchers, and
missiles bombed at the eleventh hour on the road to Benghazi
would have devastated the rebel stronghold if Qaddafi's forces had
been able to unleash them indiscriminately, as they did in other,
smaller rebel-held towns, like Zawiyah, Misrata, and Adjabiya.
Qaddafi's long track-record of arresting, torturing, disappearing,
and killing his political opponents to maintain control suggests
that had he recaptured the east, a similar fate would have awaited
those who supported the opposition there."

It may well have been, in fact, as the BBC reported, that
Obama's considered pace ended up making all the difference; "by
hanging back President Obama has forced others to take responsibility. This is not some abstract moral point. It has real consequences. The Arab League would have been loath to back a call
that America had already made. It would have made them look
like patsies for the US. If the Arab League hadn't called for a no-
fly zone it would have been easy for Russia and China to veto any
resolution."

Confronting the uncertainties inherent in the unfolding Libyan conflict, and refusing to reduce it or rationalize it into a simple choice by psychologically minimizing the perils of either course of action, and being open about his reluctance, showed true humility. And this humility itself was of tremendous value in terms of America's strategic positioning and image in the world—as MSNBC's Rachel Maddow astutely identified in her daily news show.

"Regardless of all that 'reluctant warrior . . . I want to be a peace President' talk, once they do get into office, presidential chest thumping—turning war into political capital—is an ugly but well tested art . . . The George W. Bush that ran for office in 2000 promised a humble America, a humble foreign policy, a bend over backward bias against US military intervention anywhere in the world. Lots of candidates for office promise that. A candidate by the name of Barack Obama promised that. The difference with Mr. Obama as President is that he appears to be walking more of that walk, as well as talking more of that talk . . .

"Think about the big picture here and the legacy of George W. Bush . . . Do you want the narrative of America's role in the world to be 'America leads Western aggression against Arab countries,' or don't you want that? Do you want that to continue to be the master narrative about America's role in the world or do you want the narrative to be something different? President Obama wants the narrative to be something different. He very clearly did not want this to be another American military action on the Arab world. He is very open about his reluctance . . . Why are they doing that? Because they want the narrative to change."

Obama demonstrated that he was not taking the decision to send men and women to war, and attack another Arab country, lightly. In the very way he made the decision, Obama displayed to the world an America that was not the "gung-ho aggressor" of stereotype; seeing certainties everywhere and sometimes consequently doing as much damage as it did good.

Once Obama allowed himself some time and space to tap his river of uncertainty, a number of gains began to flow from what had been a highly perilous moment. The world community acted in concert to prevent a human catastrophe and, in so doing, had recalibrated their relationships with each other. They had relearned the value of working in partnership once more, and continued to do so as the Libyan and wider upheaval rolled on. As Obama told the nation in his speech on the conflict to the National Defense University on March 28th, "Yes, this change will make the world more complicated for a time. Progress will be uneven, and change will come differently to different countries. There are places, like Egypt, where this change will inspire us and raise our hopes. And then there will be places, like Iran, where change is fiercely suppressed. The dark forces of civil conflict and sectarian war will have to be averted, and difficult political and economic concerns will have to be addressed.

The United States will not be able to dictate the pace and scope of this change. Only the people of the region can do that. But we can make a difference."

On October 20th 2011, the Gadhafi regime was toppled once and for all when Colonel Gadhafi himself was defeated and killed in his hometown of Sirte. In the battles leading up to it, Libyan forces had been enabled, but not led, by the West. After 42 years of his tyrannical rule, it was the Libyan people themselves who achieved a personal victory in overthrowing their dictator. They earned their liberation in a way that the Iraqi people had not been allowed to.

A nation was reborn and a national pride regained. And in the process, the international community had relearned the lessons of partnership, collaboration and—in a clear distinction from the Iraq venture—patience.

———

As discussed in the previous chapter, meditation is a key route through which a valuable connection to our inner world and all the vicissitudes contained within it can be achieved. If we sit in the stillness for long enough, the oscillations of our inner thoughts and uncertainties start coming into awareness, and the more we sit with them, the stronger and more resilient we become. Let's try it now . . .

INNER PARTICLE MEDITATION

Read these notes then close your eyes and take yourself gently through each step. Alternatively, you will find this guided meditation, for you to simultaneously listen to and practice, online at www.obamakarma.org/particle.html:

- Sit or stand in a comfortable position. Keep your back straight and unsupported, so you're relaxed but upright.
- Start by taking a few deep breaths and feel your lungs fill with clean air on the in-breath, and empty completely on the out-breath.
- Gently close your eyes or, if you prefer, leave them open but focused only softly on what is before you.
- Now spend a moment listening to the sounds around you, around the room and outside it. The sound of stillness, motion, noise or what ever happens to be there.

Now turn your focus within. Your inner world is a vast space. Feel that wide space within you; a space through which travels particles of dust and matter, just like the dust and mater in the air around you. All are perfectly inert and aimless. Watch them float within.

They are your thoughts and feelings and they are of all different sizes and shapes, some are fast, some are slow, some are heavy, some are light. And just like your thoughts some travel up, some down and most are generally directionless, going whichever way the air takes them.

This is the uncertainty of your inner world—going all places at once—but this is exactly as it is meant to be.

Stay with it for a few minutes. Just watch your thoughts and feelings pass by, and know the peace of knowing the real you.

• After several minutes, gradually return to the broader awareness of the room around you; imagine its features before opening your eyes, looking around and giving yourself a few moments to reorient.

Try this whenever you have a quiet moment. Even if you only have 30 seconds to yourself, close your eyes, start to focus on your breaths and watch the thoughts and emotions flow through you . . .

EMBRACE IMPERFECTION

The staff in the White House Situation Room monitor worldwide events around the clock. They serve as the ultimate filter for the leader of the free world, casting a watchful eye over the globe, occasionally sending information up the administration chain of command if and when warranted. At 5:09 AM on Friday, October 9th, 2009, they sent an email up to Robert Gibbs, the White House Press Secretary, marked "item of interest."

Shortly after, Gibbs telephoned through to the residence and woke up the President. "Mr. President, you just won the Nobel Peace Prize."

"Are you shitting me?" Obama blurted out.

"If I was do you think I'd do it like this?" Gibbs responded.

On one level it was quite inexplicable. He'd been President less than a year and even Obama himself couldn't quite figure out why he had been selected for this honor. His daughter, Malia, seemed to put things into perspective when she walked into the bedroom shortly after and announced simultaneously, "Daddy, you won the Nobel Peace Prize, and it's Bo [the White House dog]'s birthday!"

It soon began to dawn upon Obama and his team, however, that the Nobel Committee, in awarding this prize, was calling him to leadership rather than rewarding him for it. They saw a promise in him—a vision—that they wanted to encourage. It was a reward they wanted him to earn and the expectations would start with his acceptance speech. The realization of the importance of this historic address began to disseminate across the White House like ink over blotting paper. Jon Favreau, the President's chief speechwriter, hadn't checked his BlackBerry before stepping into the shower that morning, only to find forty emails buzzing frantically for his attention when he stepped out a few minutes later. "Who died?" he thought.

This was going to be an important speech. Everybody knew it. The world was waiting for direction.

Two months later in Oslo City Hall, Obama stepped up to the podium and delivered.

He began by addressing the inherent contradiction of awarding this prize for peace to the Commander-in-Chief of the military of a nation in the midst of two wars. "I'm responsible for the deployment of thousands of young Americans to battle in a distant land. Some will kill, and some will be killed. And so I come here with an acute sense of the costs of armed conflict—filled with difficult questions about the relationship between war and peace, and our effort to replace one with the other." He went on to put it into context. "War, in one form or another, appeared with the first man. At the dawn of history, its morality was not questioned; it was simply a fact, like drought or disease—the manner in which tribes and then civilizations sought power and settled their differences... We must begin by acknowledging the hard truth: We will not eradicate violent conflict in our lifetimes. There

will be times when nations—acting individually or in concert—
will find the use of force not only necessary but morally justified."

This was not remotely what the assembled audience had expected to hear so far. Some of them began shifting uncomfortably
in their seats. Was this going to be a pro-imperialist self-justifica-
tion? Obama's statement, however as it unfolded, turned out to be
far more nuanced than that.

"I make this statement mindful of what Martin Luther King
Jr. said in this same ceremony years ago: 'Violence never brings
permanent peace. It solves no social problem: it merely creates
new and more complicated ones.' As someone who stands here as
a direct consequence of Dr. King's life work, I am living testi-
mony to the moral force of non-violence. I know there's nothing
weak—nothing passive—nothing naïve—in the creed and lives
of Gandhi and King."

Obama's desire was to express the sophisticated truth—a fundamental contradiction—that lay at the heart of any debate about
war and peace:

> "So yes, the instruments of war do have a role to play in pre-
> serving the peace. And yet this truth must coexist with an-
> other—that no matter how justified, war promises human
> tragedy. The soldier's courage and sacrifice is full of glory,
> expressing devotion to country, to cause, to comrades in arms.
> But war itself is never glorious, and we must never trumpet it
> as such.
>
> "So part of our challenge is reconciling these two seem-
> ingly irreconcilable truths—that war is sometimes necessary,
> and war at some level is an expression of human folly."

War, in Obama's description, will always be inevitable but it
will also always be undesirable. As a result, the inevitability of war

should never absolve us of the responsibility to work towards peace at all times.

"Concretely, we must direct our effort to the task that President Kennedy called for long ago. 'Let us focus,' he said, 'on a more practical, more attainable peace, based not on a sudden revolution in human nature but on a gradual evolution in human institutions.'"

As he approached the end of his speech, he broadened his theme to a wider evaluation of human nature.

"We are fallible. We make mistakes, and fall victim to the temptations of pride, and power, and sometimes evil. Even those of us with the best of intentions will at times fail to right the wrongs before us.

"But we do not have to think that human nature is perfect for us to still believe that the human condition can be perfected. We do not have to live in an idealized world to still reach for those ideals that will make it a better place. The non-violence practiced by men like Gandhi and King may not have been practical or possible in every circumstance, but the love that they preached—their fundamental faith in human progress—that must always be the North Star that guides us on our journey.

"For if we lose that faith—if we dismiss it as silly or naïve; if we divorce it from the decisions that we make on issues of war and peace—then we lose what's best about humanity. We lose our sense of possibility. We lose our moral compass.

"Like generations have before us, we must reject that future. As Dr. King said at this occasion so many years ago, 'I refuse to accept despair as the final response to the ambiguities of history. I refuse to accept the idea that the 'isness' of man's present condition makes him morally incapable of reaching up for the eternal 'oughtness' that forever confronts him.'

"Let us reach for the world that ought to be—that spark of the divine that still stirs within each of our souls."

———

Through his Nobel Prize acceptance speech Obama addressed a fundamental paradox that lies at the heart of life. Whether in ourselves or in the world around us, there are always things we want to change. Obama focused on man's propensity for violence, but it can just as easily apply to any of the darker traits possessed by humanity, for example, greed or pride. We all have these flaws and imperfections within us and so does every society that has ever existed in every part of the world. Yet, at the same time, we all possess a desire to mitigate the harm that might be caused by us. No such change can ever occur, however, without first arriving at a place of acceptance. If we do not accept the inevitability of our flaws then we will never be in a position to change them. There can be no change without acceptance.

A paradox indeed.

True acceptance of our own flaws automatically creates a desire to change. In other words, there can be no acceptance without change either. Accepting the world as it is—and ourselves as we are—does not absolve us of the responsibility to change! But change that comes from a place of acceptance and love will not be forced. Instead, it will be genuine, durable and grounded in truth. The two forms of change will feel very different. Change without acceptance will be as destructive as it is constructive, whereas change emerging from acceptance will flow more naturally and benefit all.

Although the concepts of acceptance and change might seem like opposites they are in fact merely opposite sides of the same coin. A true form of one cannot exist without a true form of the other.

The implications of this lesson when considering improvement in our own lives are vast. The starting point for any personal transformation has to be acceptance. This is a lot more difficult than it sounds. In my own practice, and indeed my own life, this is always the toughest frontier.

It starts with being real about one's flaws. We all possess them. Some people only travel half the journey and stop off at a point where they can say to themselves "well, that's just the way I am so that's that." This is not true acceptance. For when we talk of our own flaws we need to realize their destructive potential, both towards ourselves and towards the world around us. Only when we realize their destructive potential, and when that realization brings forth a desire to change—do we go beyond just naming our flaws to truly accepting them.

Having accepted our flaws, we have created an automatic desire to change them. Not because we have to—but because we want to. This is a bit of a paradox as well. We know we have to change some things about ourselves—doesn't that imply "Have to"? you may ask. Not at all! True acceptance means approaching change from a loving, compassionate perspective. We love and accept ourselves the way we are, warts and all; at the same time, acknowledgement of our flaws creates a desire, a want, to change because we love ourselves and because of that love, we want to create an even better version of ourselves. In essence, when we love someone we want the best for them; that goes for ourselves as well as for others!

It is when we understand our flaws more deeply in this way that we will start to feel compelled to make positive and gradual change from a place of love.

This is an attitude that clearly drives Obama and one that he applies when building attachments and forging relationships. It is core to his *modus operandi,* and was evident even in the early days on his road to the White House.

———

It was a fault line that sat constantly beneath the surface of the Obama campaign. At any moment the tectonic plates would shift, sending an earthquake pulsating across the entire electoral landscape. Obama's friends and campaign managers all knew it would hit someday. It was just a matter of time. They tried to brace themselves, but no one could have predicted the true extent of the ultimate fallout.

March 13th, 2008 was when the quake struck. Ground zero was the Reverend Wright's Trinity United Church of Christ and his words reached 9 on the Richter Scale. His sermons of hate— equating America with the KKK, describing HIV/AIDS as a concoction of the CIA—venom beyond anything Obama had heard himself before—received round-the-clock coverage on television and radio with cable going wall-to-wall with it. The Obama campaign, which thus far had run on a message of unifying the country and transcending differences, was shaken to its foundations.

Obama himself was as disoriented as anyone else. He had never before been subjected to such an onslaught of negative press, as Fox News and their associates jumped on the bandwagon to extrapolate a ferocious stream of judgments against Obama's own character from it. In a reprise of the "swiftboating" character assassination targeted at John Kerry in the previous electoral cycle, they began to propagate the theory that Barack Obama was, in fact, a closet black radical, akin to Malcolm X or a Black Panther, whose election would certainly threaten the very union upon which the US was built. To David Axelrod, there were no two ways about it. "Do you guys understand this could be it?" he told his staff. "This could be the whole campaign . . . I don't know if we can survive this."

Within the commotion, however, Obama began to sense the bare threads of an opportunity. He had wanted to give a speech on race from the beginning of the campaign but his staff had always resisted. He knew that he was uniquely qualified to address the nation on one of its most sensitive issues, but it was too high a risk for most of the campaign high command. "A lot of folks cautioned that he had run such a transcendent race that maybe it wasn't such a good idea to introduce race," Senior Advisor Valerie Jarrett later said.

"Obama had raised giving a race speech back in the fall. At the time Axelrod and I strenuously disagreed," acknowledged David Plouffe.

But this time it was different. Obama put his foot down. "I want to give a speech on race," he told his team. "From a political standpoint, this is a moment of great peril and requires more than the typical political response. But I have got a lot to say about this and I think it requires a thoughtful speech. It's a speech that only I can write. Either people accept it or they won't, and I may not be President."

His speechwriters agitated as the day approached, they wanted to know what he was writing. "Don't worry . . . I already know what I want to say in this speech. I've been thinking about it for almost thirty years" he told them.

The day before it he sat through the night in his hotel room completing the speech himself before emailing it to the senior staff at 2 AM on the morning it was due to be delivered. Axelrod took one look at it, then emailed his boss a seven-word response. "This is why you should be President."

His speech was a master class in the power of change through acceptance; acceptance of the flaws in his pastor, acceptance of the flaws in his country, and acceptance of the flaws in even his closest family;

"I can no more disown him [Reverend Wright] than I can disown the black community. I can no more disown him than I can my white grandmother—a woman who helped raise me, a woman who sacrificed again and again for me, a woman who loves me as much as she loves anything in this world, but a woman who once confessed her fear of black men who passed her by on the street, and who on more than one occasion has uttered racial or ethnic stereotypes that made me cringe. These people are a part of me and a part of America, this country that I love."

He spoke of the flaws at the very root of his country, starting with the Declaration of Independence, which was, he believed, "stained by the nation's original sin of slavery. A question that divided the colonies and brought the convention to a stalemate."

It was through such deep acceptance that he found a connection to America's tradition of change.

"What we know—what we have seen—is that America can change. That is the true genius of this nation. What we have already achieved gives us hope—for what we can and must achieve tomorrow."

His view of his country, his community, his church and his family was not a blinkered one. He did not romanticize or idealize; instead, his view was grounded in the imperfect sheen of reality. For all their flaws he did not love them any less. He embraced them totally. And through his embrace he found his purpose: to effect change through acceptance.

————

The temptation to avoid the parts we don't like—whether in our communities, our loved ones or our selves—and embrace only those elements we do like is strong in all of us. It is easy to underestimate the real challenge of true acceptance. It is easy to turn a blind eye and pretend to deal with our flaws by sweeping them under the rug. It is easy to think the problem is "no big deal" and then essentially be blindsided by the challenge. Failure to accept what we don't like is always the first crack in any relationship, particularly in the most important relationship of all: that with ourselves.

I have seen the effects of this in the addiction clinics I once worked in. We would fashion a detoxification regime for heroin users to help wean them gradually off their opiate addiction. The program would normally consist of several stages. In the first stage we would try and cease their heroin use and replace it with methadone. This stage could take anything from a week to months or even, in some cases, years. Although the daily dose of methadone prevented the withdrawal symptoms, it would often do little for the craving for heroin they would experience on a regular basis. Once they were free from heroin, we would work with them psychologically on the cravings so they would gradually feel less and less of a pull towards the drug and, once they had worked through that sufficiently, we would start to reduce the methadone and eventually wean them off that too. I often saw patients at the beginning of their journeys and during the assessment I would describe the treatment process to them. It was in that consultation that I was usually able to predict the likely trajectory the individuals sitting before me would take, if they continued unchanged. And I would share this with them openly.

I found that those who had little patience for the first couple of stages and who came in with a desire to wean off everything instantly—including the methadone—were the ones most likely to fail. They entered the room without a full acceptance of the addictive aspect of their personalities that had led them to this juncture in the first place. They preferred to gloss over the reality of an addictive default cycle that drove them from within, when in fact an acknowledgement of this propensity would have been the first step on the road to recovery. It is only through a realistic acceptance of the full spectrum of their inner worlds—including their flaws and weaknesses—that my clients could arrive at a place of change.

In my work, I focused on facilitating this acceptance as the most important first inner step. My starting point was usually myself; I needed to start by accepting them for who they were and reflect this back to them. I did not idealize or demonize them, but instead worked hard to reflect back to them the balance of the reality that I saw before me. This sometimes made people more anxious than they were when they walked into the clinic, but it was only through that anxiety that healing could begin.

I was, of course, not the first person to discover this. Ever since the late 1930s, Alcoholics Anonymous groups—and more recently Narcotics Anonymous groups—have been springing up all over the world. Their core philosophy is based on a fundamental recognition of members' propensity towards addiction. They acknowledge that, even if they have not drunk for several years, they still contain within them the spark of addiction. It is this deep acceptance that spurs them on to change. By remaining constantly aware and vigilant of these important and undeniable aspects of their inner worlds, members are often able to maintain abstinence long after their last use.

In the same way that individuals can fall prey to addictive and self-destructive cycles, so too, from time to time, can certain facets of society, culture, religions and nations. Addressing such issues wherever they rise, at an international level, has always been a fundamental objective of foreign policy. On reaching the White House, Obama began to approach these recurring challenges through a new perspective; by applying the paradoxical principle of change through acceptance.

———

Delivering a keynote, high profile speech in a Muslim nation was always an early priority for Obama on arriving in the Oval Office. The Muslim world's view of America had taken a battering in recent years. The US's favorability rating across Muslim nations fell to lower than 20% in 2008 according to Pew's global survey. For a nation intent on building alliances with the Muslim world in order to challenge the siren calls of extremist propaganda, this was not a satisfactory state of affairs. The new administration was determined to change the relationship between America and Islam, and the starting point would be—as per Obama's play-book—acceptance.

His intention was to show his genuine respect for the Muslim world without shirking from addressing its imperfections. The opportunity was created within the first few months of his presidency when he gave his landmark address to Cairo University on June 4th, 2009.

"As a student of history, I know civilization's debt to Islam. It was Islam—at places like Al-Azhar University—that carried the light of learning through so many centuries, paving the way for Europe's Renaissance and Enlightenment. It was innovation in Muslim communities that developed the order of algebra; our magnetic compass and tools of navigation; our mastery of pens and printing; our understanding of how disease spreads and how it can be healed. Islamic culture has given us majestic arches and soaring spires; timeless poetry and cherished music; elegant calligraphy and places of peaceful contemplation. And throughout history, Islam has demonstrated through words and deeds the possibilities of religious tolerance and racial equality."

Then he segued into new terrain, addressing with fresh candor one of the most contentious subjects for Muslims globally: Israel.

"Around the world, the Jewish people were persecuted for centuries, and anti-Semitism in Europe culminated in an unprecedented Holocaust. Tomorrow, I will visit Buchenwald, which was part of a network of camps where Jews were enslaved, tortured, shot and gassed to death by the Third Reich. Six million Jews were killed—more than the entire Jewish population of Israel today. Denying that fact is baseless, ignorant, and hateful. Threatening Israel with destruction—or repeating vile stereotypes about Jews—is deeply wrong, and only serves to evoke in the minds of Israelis this most painful of memories while preventing the peace that the people of this region deserve."

Next up was another contentious issue for several corners of the Muslim world—the concern with religious freedom.

"People in every country should be free to choose and live their faith based upon the persuasion of the mind, heart, and soul. This tolerance is essential for religion to thrive, but it is being challenged in many different ways. Among some Muslims, there is a disturbing tendency to measure one's own faith by the rejection of another's."

He respected the Muslim world but would not flatter it. He wanted to be their ally in more than name, and thus he demonstrated his sincere desire to build a true relationship with them, based on reality and acceptance. This would be the foundation of a new bond.

––––––––––

The best way to change a relationship is to start from a foundation of reality, and so the key, while always being respectful, is to be open about flaws as well as strengths from the beginning. Such an approach earns more than just popularity it earns respect too. When developing a relationship, there is frequently a temptation to see only the positive platitudes and aggrandizement, but that never amounts to more than temporary elastic. The harder but ultimately far more rewarding journey is the one through acceptance and an immersion into reality. It will always be the more difficult route at first, but it is the only route through which a solid, dependable and sustainable bond can be built. Whether changing a relationship that has gone wrong, or building one anew, whether negotiating war and peace between peoples and nations, or improving marital relations between two people, the deeper the acceptance, the deeper the bond and so, over time, the deeper the change.

Accepting the world means knowing that it is an imperfect place. We cannot repair our relationship with it—and ultimately our relationship with ourselves—without first embracing the world as it is. Only through the paradoxical acceptance of imperfection, can the journey of change begin.

A key step in nurturing our "acceptance muscle," as I like to call it, is developing an appreciation for the way in which our own imperfections are actually extensions of the imperfections that exist in the world around us. Appreciating the beauty of the world around us is akin to appreciating the beauty within ourselves. Our environment affects us in the same way that the weather in any one part of the world is affected by the weather in every other. For example, our very personalities are deeply influenced by the culture into which we were born. Everything from the way we celebrate success, to the way we mourn our dead, to the way we cope with illness is substantially influenced by cultural norms. Beyond that, however, cultures can even impact the way we perceive the world around us.

People who have been raised in countries where the state oper-
ates through suppression and propaganda and shuns openness—
such as the former Soviet Bloc, for example—can develop a
mechanism of emotional suppression and distance even within
families, that might carry through generations, even for years
after the state has itself reformed its methods.

Another example is countries blighted by poverty and fear,
where that same fear and insecurity about the world can powerfully penetrate family dynamics, even after the family has immigrated away from the region.

All of this is due to the fact that we formulate our ideas about
ourselves and the world around us—who we are and how we fit
in—from our relationships with our parents in our earliest years.
If parents are suffering from the pain of traumas past, that can
easily be passed onto the toddlers they raise and, before anyone
knows it, the child will have developed whole ways of thinking
and being in the world that has incorporated that pain.

In other words, we are all the imperfect children of an imperfect world, and all the more beautiful because of it; the world is a
rich and imperfect tapestry. A deep embrace and true acceptance
of this does not leave us in a place of static despair but, instead, a
place of joyful change. Not change driven by panic or need, but
change through patience, understanding and love.

EMBRACE TO CHANGE EXERCISE

List several of your characteristics/habits that you would ide-
ally like to change. Then, next to each item describe why it is
also a characteristic that you love; it may be worthy of that
love because you understand it is born of pain or stress in
your earlier years or your present life, or you may love it

because—although it might not be good for you in the long run—it still brings you pleasure and excitement in the short term.

Finally in the 3rd column, describe why you would ultimately like to change it . . .

Characteristic/ Habit	Why I Love It . . .	Why I Want to Change It

If there are any items on this list that you really do decide to get serious about changing then I suggest you carry the words you have written around with you, and glance at them from time to time. This way, the desire to change will gradually expand within you; not with a negative or rejecting energy, but instead through love and acceptance.

As mentioned in earlier chapters, guided meditation always serves as a very powerful vehicle in the journey of self-awareness and the aim of this chapter's contemplation is to build on previous meditations, and deepen our acceptance of the diversity within ourselves and the world around us . . .

IMPERFECTION MEDITATION

Read these notes then close your eyes and take yourself gently through each step. Alternatively, you will find this guided meditation, for you to simultaneously listen to and practice, online at www.obamakarma.org/imperfection.html:

- Sit or stand in a comfortable position. Keep your back straight and unsupported, so you're relaxed but upright.
- Start by taking a few deep breaths and feel your lungs fill with clean air on the in-breath, and empty completely on the out-breath.
- Gently close your eyes or, if you prefer, leave them open but focused only softly on what is before you.
- Now spend a moment listening to the sounds around you, around the room and outside it. The sound of stillness, motion, noise or what ever happens to be there.

- Now turn your focus within. Using metaphor to open a connection to your inner world, imagine yourself as an airport terminal. Within you are all manner of people, arriving and departing all the time.
- Just like the thoughts and feelings that pass through your body, they come in all different shapes, colors and sizes. Some are weighed down with baggage, some not, some are angry, some happy, some sad, some arguing, some kissing; it's a constantly changing population of diverse people from all over the world.
- And just like you, they are all going somewhere. It is all about movement and change. Embarking on journeys and reaching destinations.

- Yet, at the same time, it is all perfect, just the way it is, and just like you. You accept it and embrace it, even though it will all change and continue to do so forever.
- Continue breathing deeply.
- As you breathe in, say to yourself "I" and as you breathe out, say to yourself "am"... "I" ... "am" ... "I" ... "am" ...
- Continue for a few minutes as you feel your whole self immersed in the perfection of an ever-changing moment.

- After several minutes, gradually return to the broader awareness of the room around you; imagine its features before opening your eyes, looking around and giving yourself a few moments to reorient.

Try this as often as you can throughout the day. Even if you only have 30 seconds to yourself, close your eyes, take a few deep breaths and start to immerse yourself in the beauty of the imperfection both within and without you.

So this tension in life—the tension between change and acceptance—surrounds us everywhere. In fact it is the engine of all achievement in the world. That is why progress always comes in waves—two steps forward and one step back. Every scientific, artistic or technological advancement made by man has been a product of this tension, gradually moving us forward in waves; with the opposing forces of our cooling fan mind, powered by the emotion of our shadow on the one hand, and the still center of acceptance and love on the other.

That is why, in order to really succeed at anything in life, we need to embrace and ride this tension. This is also a way of surfing the waves of life. Two steps forward and one step back. That's why failure is inevitable. Mistakes are inevitable. We are destined to forever undulate in this way, back and forth in both our inner and outer life. So don't ever blame yourself for screwing up. That is failure to understand yourself. Acknowledging you screwed up and blaming yourself for it are two different things. Acknowledging without blame means understanding an action within the whole context of what happened at the time and indeed your whole life leading up to it. We may sometimes act rashly or lose our tempers or do things we later wish we hadn't. Owning up to what you did wrong is fine, but the best way to ensure a repetition is to get angry about it. That is why it is so important to treat your emotional reactions in the same way you would any physical reaction.

For example, if you are cut you will bleed. You don't blame yourself for bleeding but that doesn't stop you cleaning it up. The same applies for times when you act from your ego. Know that in some way it is bound to be a factor of the pressure and stress that you experienced preceding it and so don't add to it by beating yourself up. At the same time, own up to your mistake or act to curtail it. Learn from it where possible and try to avoid it in future. Clear up your blood when it is spilt but don't get angry with yourself for having bled. That's a metaphor I often like to remind myself of when I get things wrong in my own life.

The tension of this paradox percolates into all aspects of life; staying happy with the way things are now vs. the need to improve our lot; this applies to whether or not to change our relationship, whether or not to have children, whether or not to change things about our working life, whether or not to lose weight, whether or not to aim for a better house or clothes or lifestyle. Remember, there is no right or wrong here. Both opposing forces are right—change vs. staying the same—and so both need to be honored if we are to be true to ourselves.

This way we start to recognize that our desire to improve things is just that; a desire. These are *wants* and not *needs*. There is nothing wrong with having *wants*, but *needs* can become toxic. To work towards something because we *need* it—whether it's a better car or a better relationship—we are immediately handicapping ourselves by imposing an expectation onto it. It is as if achieving it will somehow complete or rectify us. We then risk falling over ourselves in the rush to get it, and even if we do, we'll remain unfulfilled because the effect will never end up meeting the vast expectations we placed on it in the first place. To work towards something because we *want* it is a far more productive approach, because we know deep down that if we don't get it, it won't be the end of the world—because it won't affect who we really are or how we feel about ourselves—so we can go about it without so much of fuss and bother. And, paradoxically, we'll be more likely to attain our goal that way too.

LESSON **4**

MAKE SPACE FOR SHADOWS

I t was at Occidental College in Los Angeles and the year was 1979. "Pot had helped, and booze; maybe a little blow when you could afford it," admitted Obama. He had friends from black supremacist movements like the Black Panthers and even remembers berating a fellow black student for going out with a white girlfriend. Obama recalled all these moments and more with both honesty and anguish in his autobiography, yet he disowned none of them.

The most important flaws we need to accept are our own. Buddhists talk of a warrior spirit that is needed in order to face our own pain without judgment. The purpose of this next lesson is to examine and understand the part of us that we neglect the most—our shadow.

Our shadow is our dark side: the part that contains our negative thoughts, feelings, perceptions and memories. We all have them. We all feel lazy or selfish or angry or malicious at times. We are never free of this energy. And that is because we are human. The human shadow is the unique consequence of the human condition. As humans, we are all afflicted by this condition—it is both a blessing and a curse. And at its root is something we all take for granted every day of our lives: Language. The complexity of human language is something that only a species with a brain as big as ours could develop. The true value of human language is that it enables us to put together novel statements all the time. We are stringing together new meaningful sequences of words every day—sentences we have never spoken or heard before in precisely that form—(like the one I am constructing right now, for example). The reason we can do this is because each word we learn contains vast networks of meanings and associations. We can continually construct new pathways through these connections. We are so good at utilizing this brilliant tool of language that it has enabled us to grow in knowledge and creativity at an exponential pace ever since we invented it. But, there is also a dark side to language. By containing the depth of association it does, it also means that language can fool us. Take a look at this phrase for example:

RED SUNSET ON A BEACH

How does that make you feel? Take a few seconds. Stare at the words and see what comes up inside.

For most of us, it will evoke a special warm feeling, the kind of warm, peaceful presence we might experience if we are actually looking at a nice red sunset on a beach. But we're not—we're just looking at the words "red sunset on a beach" and yet that itself is enough to evoke some of those feelings in us. It's just like when you read a novel and it feels like you're watching the whole story play out before you as if you were at the movies. So the same association-based quality that enables language to be as complex and flexible as it is, also causes it to evoke a whole series of emotions within us, when in fact it's just, well, words. And these very words are what are flowing through our heads all day, every day.

With the ability to use language, has come the ability to think—i.e. use language internally—in a way that only humans can do. Our sophisticated thought process has enabled us to pursue a level of growth and creativity that has been invaluable to us as a species—otherwise we'd probably still be living in caves, as we were before we had language. But thinking doesn't end with solving problems and writing self-help books; we're thinking all the time! We can't just use our ability to think when we need it and then switch off thought when we want to go sit on the beach. We're thinking all the time. And that's pretty wasteful. Worse than that, it is actually harmful because it means that we spin all these emotion-attached words up into a frenzy inside our minds all day. This can make us happy and sad and everything in between regardless of whether or not there is actually anything in front of us to make us happy, sad, frightened, excited etc.

As a result of this ability to use language and think all the time, we possess a series of unique abilities. These include our ability to predict the future to some degree, to love romantically and to take responsibility.

Each of these is both a blessing and a curse: Our ability to predict the future enables us to plan, build and protect ourselves for the future. Our sophisticated language-fuelled minds allow us to think a few steps ahead and so act accordingly on an individual as well as a societal level. On the other hand, however, it also means we must live with the knowledge of future possible calamities, pain, illness and the inevitability of death. Animals know in the moment of danger that they may die, but it is not something they carry or contemplate years before it ever becomes a reality.

Romantic love is also a true gift. We can think about, contemplate and escalate our love for days on end without even seeing the object of our affection. But at the same time—anybody who has experienced love will tell you—it possesses its own unique pain and stress too; countless plays have been staged, books written and songs sung to attest the yearnings and pain we also feel when experiencing the ups and downs of a relationship.

Our ability to take responsibility means we can be charged with our own unique role in the world, whether in work or family life. We can solve problems and achieve things and it leaves us feeling empowered, needed and worthwhile. We feel good about meeting an objective long after the day of achievement has passed. But on the other hand, failure to deliver on the promise of that responsibility, as inevitably happens from time to time in a world we cannot fully control, means we will also suffer a sense of failure and guilt when things don't work out. And our thinking brains won't let us forget it, either, for days, weeks, sometimes months and years afterwards.

So a lot of the negative thoughts, feelings and attitudes that constitute the shadow are a consequence of our large brains' ability to both use and abuse language. That's the uniquely human aspect of our shadow.

In addition to this, our shadow possesses a couple of older, yet profoundly powerful, elements we share in common with virtually all living beings; the drives to survive/compete and procreate. There is within us the constant desire to "do better" and "go higher," defeat the opponent and vanquish the enemy. It can carry us away to sometimes extreme, harmful and violent levels, or push us all the way in the opposite direction towards pessimism and apathy. And the same goes for our drive to procreate, pushing us to potentially unhealthy excess in the sexual sphere, too. Any of these drives, if left unchecked, can lead to addictions in their own right; to wealth, success, power or sex—particularly with the fuel of our language-driven mind egging us on from behind. All of us can sometimes feel like we're just a few small steps away from spiraling out of control.

Add all this together and we are left with an array of factors fuelling our shadow, leading to fear, agitation, guilt, jealousy, irritation, rivalry, you name it—all lurking within us, beneath the surface, at any particular moment.

All this is inevitable.

The shadow arises the very second we are born. The first thing a baby does when it leaves the womb is let out a huge cry. The fear that comes with the very act of being born into the world is something we can never escape. The first experience of separateness is an earth-shattering shock, and the needs of a baby at that moment are complete and total. Anything less than 100% attention, 100% of the time will lead the baby to experience ongoing fear and need. Yet, no parent could ever satisfy this demand and as a result, every child will begin to grow something akin to a black hole inside of unmet need. We all have it. This is the foundation upon which our shadow will be built year after year.

Now when we are children we can usually express a lot of the accumulating pain in the instant we feel it. As I mentioned, the first thing we do upon being born is scream. In the early days and months the hungry or angry child lets anyone in his presence know how he feels that instant. But as we grow older, we start to learn that we can't do that anymore—or if we did, we wouldn't get very far as social beings. As a result, we learn, appropriately, to keep a lot of the frustration that life inevitably brings us, inside. It doesn't externalize, so instead it builds up within. Hour by hour, day by day. This is the rise of the shadow. And as we learn language, we learn new and inventive ways to churn and retain this pain, effectively turning our shadow into a high-interest pain bank.

In some ways, however, the shadow actually goes back to before our own birth: Each of us is affected in a unique way by the dynamic that builds up between ourselves and our parents, and in this way our parents' shadow actually affects the development of our own. Our parents themselves carry the shadows and burdens that have been built up within them over their lifetimes, and their own shadows have, in turn, been passed on from their own parents. That is how whole cultures and regions can contain a series of traumas within the shadow that get passed on from generation to generation and the cause may go back decades or even centuries to events—wars, famine, abuse—that have long since passed.

Through our journey of life we will always be affected by the shadow of those around us too: friends, partners and colleagues. Indeed it is our shadow that connects us to the whole of humanity. That is why it is essential, wherever possible, to avoid judgment of it, whether in ourselves or in others. The shadow is part of the tangled complexity that makes each of us what we are and so to attempt to disown or judge it would be as futile as attempting to detach the skin from our bodies. The key to healing is actually awareness of our shadow, without judgment. Such awareness is easier at the feeling level than at the level of words and thought, for the very words we use to refer to it, like "dark side," "shadow," "negatives," "flaws" are laden with judgment. The best attitude is that of a small child, a pure observer, unable to attach any thoughts or ideas to what she sees. We can feel without judgment; whether the pain of ourselves or the pain of others. It is only after we attempt to translate that to words or definitions that the need to form a judgment creeps in.

Because we're not used to just experiencing our emotions in this way—just noticing, rather than labeling them—we often allow them to slip under our radar of consciousness and into the darkness of the subconscious. It is in the darkness that the shadow thrives and really starts to grow. If we always strive to bring our shadow into awareness, but without judgment, we are taking important steps to improve ourselves. Indeed the very act of judgment of our shadow is itself a manifestation of it. For example we will often realize that we have been in some way wrong, inattentive, selfish or unfair in a particular situation, and that we need to change our approach to rectify things. In other words, this is a moment at which we have developed a new awareness of a manifestation of our shadow. The most common and surefire way to invite the shadow back in and expand it again is if we then start to judge ourselves for getting it wrong in the first place!

So awareness is the key. Even awareness of the fact that we will not always be aware, for if we were, then there would be no shadow in the first place. And if there were no shadow, then there would be no us.

It takes us back to the lesson of the previous chapter. The only way to truly change is to start from acceptance. This fundamental paradox at the core of life applies to our most primal aspect: our shadow. Only after we learn to accept and embrace the shadow within us for what it is, requiring no change or evolution, will it begin to shift a little. By becoming aware of it, accepting and respecting it, we deactivate it a bit. And that's all we need to do. We will never deactivate it entirely, nor should we. Every light has a shadow, and the moment we find ourselves thinking we have eradicated the shadow we have, in fact, become overwhelmed by it.

During his campaign for president, Obama promised the most open and transparent government in history. The vision was clear and the determination unequivocal; throwing open the doors of Washington was a key priority, and he consistently talked of a new way of doing business. He even went as far as to draw a picture of how things would look when he was in charge. "I'm going to have all the negotiations around a big table," Obama said on healthcare, for example. "We'll have doctors and nurses and hospital administrators. Insurance companies, drug companies— they'll get a seat at the table, they just won't be able to buy every chair. But what we'll do is we'll have the negotiations televised on C-SPAN, so that people can see who is making arguments on behalf of their constituents and who are making arguments on behalf of drug companies or the insurance companies."

As promised, healthcare was indeed an early priority for his administration and so, from the start, this would be prime terrain in which he could demonstrate his vision for open government. What was also pressing at the time, however, was the need to actually succeed in drafting legislation that would, for the first time in history, provide healthcare coverage to most of the forty million Americans who had none. As the stop-start legislative battles wore on, the possibility of total failure—as had befallen Bill Clinton's healthcare reform plan in 1994—reared its head time and time again. Obama's focus increasingly narrowed to the endgame and securing the legislation once and for all. Transparency started falling by the wayside. The public fretted as one round of talks after another took place behind closed doors. On October 27th, 2009 Chris Frates wrote in *Politico* that:

"In recent weeks, negotiations, particularly in the Senate, have been anything but open. Senate Majority Leader Harry

Reid (D-Nev.) and Sens. Max Baucus (D-Mont.) and Chris
Dodd (D-Conn.) have been meeting with top White House
aides to draft the bill Reid will bring to the Senate floor. The
private talks have been held around Reid's conference table,
and participants have been tight-lipped about the proceed-
ings.

"After the first meeting, reporters chased Rahm Emanuel
as he walked from Reid's office to visit Speaker Nancy Pelosi,
but the White House chief of staff didn't disclose any details
of what was discussed.

"In a press briefing last week, White House press secretary Robert Gibbs also said nothing about what's being decided behind closed doors."

Soon, and perhaps as a consequence, the deals that started to
come out of these conclaves began to look increasingly unsavory;
the kind of agreements that would never have been reached had
the meetings in which they were drafted ever seen the light of day.
Senator Ben Nelson, who was always a wavering vote on the issue,
asked for special dispensation for his state. All states would be
required to pay for an expansion in Medicaid, but his state—Nebraska—would be exempted. Instead, the rest of the country
would subsidize Nebraska's expansion. This would amount to
$45 million dollars for the first decade alone.

The Republicans had a field day with it. John McCain chris-
tened it "The Cornhusker Kickback" in the Senate. "The Federal
Government will now fund Nebraska's new Medicaid recipients
forever . . . yes folks, forever!!"

Another deal was mocked as "The Louisiana Purchase." In
return for another wavering vote—that of Louisiana Senator
Mary Landrieu—around $100 million for extra Medicare subsi-
dies would be paid to her state.

Deals such as this helped the Republicans whip the public up into increasing fervor against what was going on in their government, but it only seemed to push the Obama team to shut the doors tighter in their increasingly frantic efforts to garner Congressional votes. Melanie Sloan, executive director of Citizens for Responsibility and Ethics in Washington, formerly a supporter of Obama's proposals for more open government, spoke out. She believed that Obama had a duty, if not to conduct the meetings in public, at least to brief the public about what was going on inside the meetings.

David Axelrod, who had weekly strategy meetings at his home with old friends from the world of political consulting and polling, found himself surrounded by calls to at least campaign more clearly on the issues being discussed. "This is a campaign." One told him. But Axelrod, at the time, would have none of it. They were in governing mode and they had to get the job done. Briefing and campaigning would come later. "Well, tell that to the other side," a former colleague pitched in. "They're running a campaign!"

Though they were undoubtedly sincere in their desire to change the nation for the better and improve the lives of tens of millions of Americans, the very goal-directed drive that was moving them forward was also pushing them into a bunker. The same energy that was fuelling their progress was also creating a shadow, and openness and transparency became the casualties. Obama's focus on one area led him to take the eye off the ball in another. The tone that was created then put off a swath of voters, particularly independents who weren't so sure about what kind of leader Obama was anymore and, as a result, became more receptive to the anti-Obama messages coming from the other side.

The same push that ultimately led to the passing of historic legislation, achieving healthcare for tens of millions of Americans, also led Obama to abandon the much cherished promise of a more visible and less secretive government at the same time. This ultimately lit the fuse that seriously damaged the Democratic Party in the 2010 Congressional elections, when over sixty Democratic lawmakers lost their seats, and the party lost control of the House of Representatives—something unthinkable only months earlier.

With every ray of light comes a shadow.

A key consequence of being disconnected from our shadow is that we start to project those attributes onto other people. Projection was a concept coined by Freud and basically means that the bits of us we can't handle, we throw onto others. Picture it as a kind of dough. Once it is affixed to another person, it becomes less unsettling for us to observe and easier still to judge. It is something all of us do. The parts of our shadow that remain unconscious are projected onto the outside world so we end up seeing them in all manner of places; passersby, friends, relatives, partners, even whole races of people.

It also works the other way around too. Projection is the prime means by which the shadow of others—particularly our parents, partners and those closest to us—is also passed on to us. By planting a series of unwanted negatives on us in their own minds' eyes, they can lead us to a point where we start to internalize the criticism until finally it might just become a part of our own shadow. Whereas all along, it was simply a facet of their own insecurity. That is how shadows pass from generation to generation and from one partner to another. There are many facets of my own shadow I can trace back to my parents' shadows, and their forefathers too. But that does not mean that we can blame or judge someone for projecting onto us. This is because it is a human reflex. Projection is as natural to us as going into an adrenaline-charged, fight-flight mode in response to a threat. Though we must always be on guard for it, we will nevertheless always do it. Acknowledging and accepting its inevitability should not, however, absolve us of the responsibility to keep it in check whenever we can. Change through acceptance. I do it with myself all the time. Whenever I feel judgment bubbling up inside me for a person, I sit with it and use it as an opportunity to connect more deeply with myself.

Projection is a major part of relationships. Whenever we argue—particularly when it is a passionate argument—there are often projections flying around, both ours and the other person's. That's not to say that someone's criticism of you is always wrong or that you are always wrong to criticize another person, but frequently we or they will overdo it, and when we do, that's when projection has hitched a ride.

Exploring these things is, for me, the most precious gift of a relationship. This is the difference between a relationship of true love and something more superficial. When we first meet someone there are plenty of gaps for us to fill in with our own creativity; we may believe them to possess all sorts of attributes and qualities that are in fact, merely figments of our own imaginations—projections too, although positive ones at first. Soon, however, we begin to brush up against their shadow, and they brush up against ours. Before we know it, we are projecting those aspects onto each other too and so each of us perceives in the other a combination of their own attributes plus our own shadow. Things can then go one of two ways; either we reject what we see (and when the relationship becomes toxic, there is sometimes no alternative to this), or we work with it—recognizing and reuniting with our own shadow through them. Over time, as we grow and start to embrace our own shadow—through seeing it reflected in them—we can find ourselves growing stronger and more able to embrace theirs too. And, often we will find that theirs is not dissimilar to our own. After all it is quite common that the pains within our shadows are what brought us together in the first place.

By learning to love yourself—warts and all—you can learn to love another, and by learning to love another, you will learn to love yourself too.

Every relationship, whether with a partner, or a work colleague or even with a complete stranger, offers us the possibility of reuniting with our shadow. The next exercise demonstrates a practical way in which we can work towards this on a day-to-day basis.

PROJECTION EXERCISE

Whenever you find yourself judging someone in your head; whether it is someone you have noticed on a bus because of their slightly unusual appearance or a friend, partner, colleague or relative, start by exploring the feeling you are having towards them. Are you judging an action or a behavior, or is your feeling more akin to judging them as a person?—i.e. "he is dumb," rather than "what he did then was dumb." Judging a person rather than an act means it is likely you are adding something about the way you feel towards yourself into the picture. So, in this example, it could be that a part of you feels yourself to be in some way dumb underneath it all. Not that you are, mind. It's just that on some level, you feel that way.

This exercise is as much a feeling one as it is a thinking one. Whenever such a judgment seems to be surfacing, then,

pause a minute and **TAME** your projection by going through
the following steps:

Take back the projection

Accept it, as your own issue

Meld with it (feel how it feels when it's back inside you)

Embrace it—do not reject or shun it. Know that it is a part
of you, as worthy of love as any other, and likely born from a
cycle of projection that predates even your own existence.

After a while this will become a habit. Then, every time you
start to judge someone as a person—and there will always be
such times, remember, projection is a natural human reflex
we will always engage in—you will, nevertheless, have turned
it from a self-destructive cycle into a cycle of growth; a way
to reconnect more deeply with yourself.

I once went to a weekend retreat led by a former Buddhist
monk. We all sat quietly in the hall as he arrived and took his
position on the small stage. He sat in the lotus position, looked
around the audience before him and smiled. It was a gentle, loving smile and I waited to hear his tales of Bliss and Nirvana and
how to achieve it. But as he began to talk he veered down a totally
unexpected track. "I have been depressed," he told us. "Sometimes, I have been so depressed and negative that I have just laid
there in bed thinking nothing good will ever happen to me again."

I looked on aghast. *What have I signed myself up for?*

In fact, the weekend turned out to be one of the most enlight-
ening of my life.

The speaker had been a monk for nearly two decades and
reached quite a senior position. So much so that he realized his

life was becoming a little too cushioned and privileged. He was well known throughout the Buddhist world, was given assistants, was picked up from airports in limousines and received praise, respect, copious food and top-notch board wherever he went. As a result he found himself reconnected with a yearning to return to a more simple, anonymous life. One day, after much anguish and thought, he finally took the plunge, defrocked, gave it all up, and returned to the wide unknown world again.

He talked openly about his doubts and the stress, anxiety and sheer panic he sometimes felt as a result. He did not shrink from sharing with us his dark side. It was as if the whole weekend was designed to convey to us the message that, "just like you, I have all sorts of issues, angers, fears and anguish going on inside me all the time." He was open about losing his temper in traffic and swearing at bad drivers, just like the rest of us. He talked about a revered Buddhist teacher of his who would feel so lousy some mornings that he once remembers waking up and saying to himself, "may all sentient beings go to hell!"

Another monk I once heard of traveled to California to teach students there about loving kindness and the compassionate spirit of Buddhism. Yet, at the end of each day, he would come home filled with disgust at the students' lax and ill-disciplined lifestyles. He would cry each night at what he thought was his own failure to possess the very compassion he was preaching to them.

The point of the weekend was to teach us that compassion starts at home. It is only after we gain compassion for our own shadow—our own negative, dark, anguished and fearful side—that we can have it for others. The notion is encapsulated well in the title of a book I once heard a psychiatrist colleague was working on, called *I'm Not OK, You're Not OK, But That's OK.*

One of my favorite writers, Pema Chödrön, put it beautifully: "It isn't that one is the bad part and one is the good part, but it's a

kind of interesting smelly, rich, fertile mess of stuff. When it's all
mixed up together, it's us; humanness... Both the brilliance and
the suffering are here for all time. They interpenetrate each other.
For a fully enlightened being, the difference between what is neurosis and what is wisdom is very hard to perceive, because somehow the energy underlying both of them is the same." She goes on
to say, "our hang ups, unfortunately or fortunately, contain our
wealth. Our neurosis and our wisdom are made out of the same
material. If you throw out your neurosis you also throw out your
wisdom. Someone who is very angry also has a lot of energy.
That's the reason people love that person. The idea isn't to get rid
of your anger but to make friends with it, to see it clearly with
precision and honesty and also to see it with gentleness. That
means not judging yourself as a bad person but also not bolstering
yourself up by saying 'It's good that I'm this way, it's right that I'm
this way. Other people are terrible, and I'm right to be so angry at
them all the time.' The gentleness involves not repressing the
anger, but also not acting it out. It is something much softer and
more open-hearted than any of that."

This is all from her book *The Wisdom of No Escape* which I
thoroughly recommend. It grabbed me early on when she started
by describing the lineage of the inspirational and respected monks
who had led the particular Buddhist tradition she followed, and
before whose images she bowed each day:

"It is sometimes called the 'mishap lineage' because of the
ways in which the wise and venerated teachers of this lineage
'blew it' time after time. First there was Tilopa. A madman,
completely wild. His main student was Naropa. Naropa was
so conceptual and intellectual that it took him twelve years of
being run over by a truck, of being put through all sorts of
trials by his teacher, for him to begin to wake up. He was so

conceptual that if somebody would tell him something, he
would say. 'Oh yes, but surely, by that you must mean this.'
He had that kind of mind. His main student was Marpa,
who was famous for his intensely bad temper. He used to fly
into rages, beat people and yell at them. He was also a drunk.
He was notorious for being incredibly stubborn. . . . Marpa
became a student of the dharma because he thought he could
make a lot of money bringing texts back from India and
translating them into Tibetan."

But, Chödrön tells us, they were nothing compared to what
came next. Marpa's student was Milarepa. "Milarepa was a murderer! . . . Milerpa became a student because he was afraid he was
going to hell for having murdered people—that scared him."

From this, she concludes, "We could all take heart. These are
the wise ones who sit in front of us. To whom we prostrate when
we do prostrations. We can prostrate to them as an example of our
own wisdom mind of enlightened beings, but perhaps it's also
good to prostrate to them as confused, mixed-up people with a lot
of neurosis, just like ourselves. They are good examples of people
who never gave up on themselves and were not afraid to be themselves who, therefore, found their own genuine quality and their
own true nature."

We all have darkness and light within us. We all have a
shadow; you do just as I do too. Indeed, the very energy that created my shadow led me to write this book, and the very energy
that created your shadow is leading you to read this book too.
And if you are growing half as much by reading it as I am by
writing it, then it is yet another example of why we should be
thankful for our shadows. For it is our shadows that make us who
we are.

SHADOW MEDITATION

Read these notes then close your eyes and take yourself gently through each step. Alternatively, you will find this guided meditation, for you to simultaneously listen to and practice, online at www.obamakarma.org/shadow.html:

- Sit or stand in a comfortable position. Keep your back straight and unsupported, so you're relaxed but upright.
- Start by taking a few deep breaths and feel your lungs fill with clean air on the in-breath, and empty completely on the out-breath.
- Gently close your eyes or, if you prefer, leave them open but focused only softly on what is before you.
- Now spend a moment listening to the sounds around you, around the room and outside it. The sound of stillness, motion, noise or what ever happens to be there.

- Now bring your focus to the shadow within. The dark, heavy energy of your shadow, which you carry around with you all the time. The weight is forever present and unavoidable. As you breathe in, feel your shadow enter your lungs and your heart through your nose.
- This shadow is connected to all mankind through the shadows of all the rest of humanity and so, as you breathe in your own shadow, you are breathing in all shadows of all people.
- Feel it fill your lungs, you heart and your chest.
- Then breathe out the opposite energy—an energy of peace, lightness and space. Breathe it out to yourself and the rest of the world.

- Continue gently taking deep breaths, inhaling the shadow in, and exhaling peace, space and light outwards.
- You are connected to all through your shadow. You are connected to peace through your shadow. You are one with all. And you resist nothing.
- Continue this exercise for several minutes.

- After several minutes, gradually return to the broader awareness of the room around you; imagine its features before opening your eyes, looking around and giving yourself a few moments to reorient.

Try this whenever you can throughout the day. Just close your eyes, and breathe your shadow in and peace out.

LESSON 5

CONNECT TO YOUR CORE

The year was 1988. Mary Andersen was a 31 year-old new-lywed, waiting excitedly in line at a check-in counter in Miami airport, bound for Norway to join her new hus-band. It was the first step in the next chapter of her life. Filled with expectation and excitement, she had packed all of her be-longings in preparation for her immigration to her new home. She reached the counter, expecting everything to run smoothly, when she was suddenly stopped in her tracks by the check-in staff. They informed her that the weight of her luggage meant she would need to pay an extra $103 surcharge. Mary had no money and had no one else she could call. The airline staff remained unsympathetic and, though she pleaded, they were unbending.

For Mary, there seemed to be no way out. She began to cry. All her plans seemed to be falling apart. "Tears were pouring down my face and I had no idea what to do," she recalled. The staff was about to move her aside to serve the next passengers. "Then I heard a gentle and friendly voice behind me saying, 'That's OK, I'll pay for her.'" Mary turned around to see a tall man whom she had never seen before. He had a gentle and kind voice, but his demeanor was firm and decisive. Two decades later a Norwegian newspaper reported the story; "Although this happened 20 years ago, Mary still remembers the authority that radiated from the man."

He was just a 27 year-old law student. Mary watched over the years, however, as the kindly stranger she once met became an American Senator, then the Democratic Party nominee and eventually the 44th President of the United States.

Once in the White House, Obama was intent on making sure that he kept in regular contact with ordinary people. He was acutely aware of the dangers of living in a bubble and potentially becoming emotionally detached as a result. This is why he appointed someone he knew and trusted personally to head up one of the least known, but most vital areas of his administration; the White House Office of Presidential Correspondence. Mike Kelleher had known Obama from his early Chicago days when they both ran for Congress together—and failed—in the 1990s. Kelleher went on to work for Obama in Chicago and then continued on his Senate staff in Washington. Their long association meant that Obama could trust him to do a job he valued highly. Kelleher's prime responsibility was to supervise the sifting of the thousands of letters that arrived at the White House each day and present ten every morning to the President. Obama read each and responded to many personally. He believed this to be an essential part of his day. It kept him grounded. In addition to the stories he read in the daily batch of letters, he also spent time after most public events, talking to the attendees one-to-one to hear their stories too. One such person was Laura Klitzka. She was a young mother of two in Green Bay, Wisconsin and she introduced Obama at a high school event, five months into his presidency.

Laura had terminal breast cancer and her medical bills were going unpaid. In his book *Revival* Richard Wolffe describes the exchange. "Laura... had undergone eight rounds of chemotherapy and thirty-three rounds of radiation as well as a double mastectomy. That treatment failed to stop the cancer from spreading to her bones. Even with her husband's insurance, Laura faced more than $12,000 in unpaid medical bills, and resorted to paying her mortgage with a credit card. She said she didn't want to waste the little time she had with her children in worrying about her unpaid medical bills. Yet Laura's simple smile, her matter-of-fact delivery, and her singsong upper Midwestern accent gave little hint of her suffering. Obama walked to the microphone and thanked Laura for sharing her story. 'It takes courage to do that, and it takes even more courage to battle a disease like cancer with such courage and determination, and I know her family is here and they're working and fighting with her every inch of the way.'" Obama was visibly moved.

Later that day David Axelrod presented him with polling data, underlining the stark political perils for him in plowing full speed ahead with healthcare reform. Progress thus far had been limited and the omens looked even worse. "This is going to be costly." He warned his boss, "You need to know that."

"I'm sure you're right." Obama responded after hearing him out patiently. "But I just got back from Green Bay where I met a woman. She's thirty-five years old and has two children, and she's got breast cancer. They're going broke because the insurance won't cover most of her treatment. She's terrified that she's going to die and leave her family bankrupt. So you know, the fight is worth it." He walked Axelrod to the door, "we have to keep going."

Compassion is at the core of who we are; every single one of us. In recent years a wealth of evidence has converged from the worlds of psychology, evolutionary biology, sociology and anthropology to show that the human race actually evolved less through "survival of the fittest" and more through a form of "survival of the kindest."

Studies are showing that it is the compassionate instinct that has enabled groups to survive by supporting each other, and so provide an advantage to the species. Evolution has led compassion to become hardwired into our systems and this has now been demonstrated through a variety of studies across several areas of our functioning. For example, in research by Emory University neuroscientists James Rilling and Gregory Berns, participants were given the chance to perform altruistic tasks to help someone else, while their brain activity was being recorded. What Rilling and Berns found was that helping others triggered activity in exactly the same regions of the brain that start firing when we receive rewards or experience pleasure directly ourselves. So helping others gives us the same pleasure and stimulation as helping ourselves!

Indeed it has also been found that, just as there is a programmed physiological response to external threats in our bodies—i.e. the fight-flight response—so there is an equally powerfully programmed response to situations that require compassion. In other words, we are as hardwired to be compassionate to others when the need arises, as we are to protect ourselves when danger arises. In addition, we even possess a hormone—oxytocin—whose virtually sole role, when released within us, is to promote feelings of nurturing and warmth toward others; the basis of compassion.

It is no coincidence that the world's great religions also con-
verge around this central theme of compassion: Christianity
evokes compassion as an essential virtue. The Bible is filled with
stories of Christ's compassion towards people that society had
shunned, whether due to their social status—the poor, the desti-
tute—or due to illnesses, that others avoided contact with. He
frequently tends to the suffering and the bereaved, and the Gos-
pels promote compassion through parables such as the tale of the
Good Samaritan in the gospel of Luke. In the Gospel of Mat-
thew, the apostle Peter tells us, "Finally be ye all of one mind,
having compassion, one of another, love as brethren, be pitiful, be
courteous."

For Judaism, a fundamental mitzvoth (commandment described in the Torah) is to emulate God in his attribute of compassion. Other mitzvoths include "love thy neighbor as thyself" and,
"be kind to a stranger, for you were strangers in the land of
Egypt." Elsewhere is the Jewish concern for "Tzedakah" (charity)
and indeed, it is said that the entire attitude of the religion is sum-
marized within the story of the Jewish scholar, Hillel. Hillel was
asked by a Roman soldier to summarize Judaism "while standing
on one foot" i.e. in a nutshell. He responded by repeating Judaism's original Golden Rule: "That which is hateful to yourself, do
not do unto others. That is the heart of the Torah. All the rest is
commentary."

Compassion is also a very prominent aspect of Islam, though
this is often little known outside the religion itself. The word *rahman*—meaning compassionate—is frequently peppered throughout the Koran and it is one of the most commonly used names of
Allah: al-rahman al-rahim, meaning the compassionate and the
merciful. It is said that "rahman" embraces all that exists in the
universe. One of the five pillars of Islam is to give Zakat; charity.

The Koran states, "Zakat is only for the poor and the needy, and those employed to administer it." Also, the major purpose of the Muslim holy month of Ramadan is to increase ones awareness of the hunger of others and thus develop sensitivity to the suffering others may face in this world.

Loving kindness and the development of compassion are, of course, fundamental goals of Buddhist practice in all its forms. The Dalai Lama addresses the issue in virtually every one of his talks and interviews. "Love and compassion are necessities not luxuries, without them humanity cannot survive," he tells us, and, "If you want others to be happy, practice compassion. If you want to be happy, practice compassion."

Like Buddhism, Christianity delivers a vivid message of compassion through pain. Christ's crucifixion is seen as an act of compassion for all humanity's sins. For me, there is a powerful parallel here for each of us. In some way there is a Christ within us all, feeling the pain of the world's suffering. For it is through our own shadow and our pain that we can connect with the rest of mankind. It is from this shared experience of pain that we develop the ability to have compassion for one another. Inwardly we realize that none of us are all that different from anyone else; "there but for the grace of God go I" is one of my favorite sayings.

So all compassion must start within. Here, again, science provides further corroboration: There is a body of research that shows that high levels of self-compassion leads to fewer symptoms of anxiety and depression, and higher overall quality of life. Self-compassion is defined primarily as the ability to take responsibility for our misgivings but, at the same time, to be accepting of our flaws and so extend kindness towards ourselves during difficult times. It is not the same as self-pity, where we blame the world for our unhappiness; self-compassion is about accepting our own share of the blame whenever things go wrong, without judging ourselves for it—in other words, embracing our humanness.

Compassion is never a one-way street. We can neither give nor receive compassion alone. Both giving and receiving must co-exist. An increase in one requires an increase in the other and vice versa. Before you can love someone else, you must first be able to love yourself.

You may have noticed that so far, the course has focused on our humanness—our uncertainties, our imperfections, our frailties and our shadows—those parts of us we have the greatest difficulty embracing. But, we have learned, it is only through such an embrace that we can find happiness. Our pain and shadows are no less important than what we consider to be our positive attributes.

As Pema Chödrön puts it, compassion towards ourselves means: "We can still be crazy after all these years. We can still be angry after all these years. We can still be timid or jealous or full of feelings of unworthiness . . . It's about befriending who we are already . . . a process of lightening up, of trusting the basic goodness of what we have and who we are, and realizing that any wisdom that already exists, exists in what we already have. Our wisdom is all mixed up with what we call neurosis. Our brilliance, our juiciness, our spiciness, is all mixed up with our craziness and our confusion."

Once we are able to embrace "our craziness" we will find it a lot easier to do the same with others. Our expectations will never be unrealistic, because we see the humanness in all of us.

This is where meditation comes in. It is simply the best method there is to find that peace with ourselves. Again, Chödrön's words are invaluable here; "When we are sitting in meditation we are simply exploring humanity and all of creation in the form of ourselves. We can become the world's greatest experts on anger, jealousy and self-depreciation, as well as on joyfulness, clarity and insight. Everything that human beings feel we feel. We can become extremely wise and sensitive to all of humanity and the whole universe, simply by knowing ourselves, just as we are."

COMPASSION MEDITATION

Read these notes then close your eyes and take yourself gently through each step. Alternatively, you will find this guided meditation, for you to simultaneously listen to and practice, online at www.obamakarma.org/compassion.html:

- Sit or stand in a comfortable position. Keep your back straight and unsupported, so you're relaxed but upright.
- Start by taking a few deep breaths and feel your lungs fill with clean air on the in-breath, and empty completely on the out-breath.
- Gently close your eyes or, if you prefer, leave them open but focused only softly on what is before you.
- Now spend a moment listening to the sounds around you, around the room and outside it. The sound of stillness, motion, noise or what ever happens to be there.

- Now turn your focus within. Using metaphor to open a connection to your inner world, imagine inside you is a school playground. Small children run around the playground. They play with one another in groups, some alone, some in pairs. Some laugh, some cry, some argue, some shout, some try and sneak out, some run or walk in. The whole gamut is inside you.

- This is you—your thoughts and feelings: Some are hurtful, some are pleasant, some are fearful, and some are serious.
- Allow yourself to be with what is. Whatever comes up, just sit with it.
- Watch your moods, thoughts and feelings run here and there like the children in the playground.
- As you do, know that it's OK. This is how you are. This is who you are. This is how all of humanity is—large and small, old and young—and you are a unique manifestation of it, as beautiful as every other.
- Like a ray of sunlight, feel your love and compassion shine across the little children—the thoughts, urges and feelings—within you.
- The sunlight comes from your core, and your compassionate heart is your core.
- Sit now for a few minutes feeling the glare of compassion, emanating from your heart, across the whole of your ever-busy inner world.

- After several minutes, gradually return to the broader awareness of the room around you; imagine its features before opening your eyes, looking around and giving yourself a few moments to reorient.

Try this whenever it feels right throughout the day. Even if you only have 30 seconds to yourself; close your eyes, take a few deep breaths and start to immerse yourself in the compassion of your heart, then send it out to the world around you.

2011 was a year like no other in his presidency. With a Republican-dominated House of Representatives, Obama was no longer free to pursue the agenda he wanted but was instead embroiled in a quagmire of budget battles. After narrowly avoiding a federal government shutdown on two occasions—with negotiations running to the wire on each—Obama and Congress hardly enjoyed a moment's breathing space before the next big battle stirred into view: The raising of the debt ceiling.

Every so often, as long as the government remains in debt, Congress needs to vote to raise the debt ceiling. It is not a vote anyone likes, but it is essential for the continued functioning of government and the economy. A failure to raise the debt ceiling is the equivalent of the government refusing to pay its credit card bills. Such an event would send a catastrophic panic across the markets, resulting in a run on government bonds, which would paralyze the government's ability to raise any credit or trade in futures and bring it to a virtual standstill.

Obama understandably wanted the routine vote to increase the debt ceiling to go ahead without controversy, but his Republican opponents had other ideas. They wanted concessions from Obama in return. What emboldened them particularly was the example of a young Democratic Senator who had voted against raising the debt ceiling only a few short years ago, when George W. Bush was in power. His name? Barack Obama.

Knowing his own record had become the Republican's sharpest weapon, Obama stepped forward and came clean. "President Barack Obama regrets his vote against raising the debt ceiling when he was a Senator and George W. Bush was President," White House press secretary Jay Carney said. With candor, he acknowledged his past folly. "He realizes now that raising the debt ceiling is so important to the health of this economy and the

global economy that it is not a vote that even when you are protesting the administration's policies you can play around with."

Clearly Obama's vote in 2006 was not his finest hour, indeed
some had come to regard it as reckless, and certainly, sitting in the
Oval Office, Obama himself had come to realize the gravity of his
mistake. Yet it is the way he then handled this knowledge of certain error on his part that is most intriguing.

As his Press Secretary's statement shows, Obama was clearly
not shrinking from taking responsibility for his past action, nor
was he minimizing it. Yet during an interview with George
Stephanopoulos on ABC on April 14th, Obama revealed a glimpse
of how he saw himself and his actions on this matter.

"It's important to realize the vantage point of a senator, versus
the vantage point of a president. When you're a senator, this is always a lousy vote . . . But as president, you start realizing that we
can't play around with this stuff. This is the full faith and credit
of the United States." He told Stephanopoulos. "That was an example of a new Senator making a political vote, rather than doing
something that was important for the country. And I'm the first
one to acknowledge it."

He was admitting, openly and unequivocally, to having put
politics before what was, in policy terms, right for the country.
This was clearly a transgression and there was no getting around
it. Yet, despite the fact that the actions of the younger Obama
were clearly out of sync with the Obama in the Oval Office, he
displayed a genuine understanding toward himself: He put it in
context. He did not beat himself up. He openly appreciated how
his vantage was a consequence of his position at the time. It wasn't
right, but he understood it. It was his ability to give himself this
kind of nuanced break—rather than descend into a morass of
self-recrimination or erect a fortress of self-denial—that gave him

the permission to brush himself off, learn from his past mistakes and continue to do what he believed was right.

Through this compassion for himself, in all his shades, he was able to stay connected to his core and continue to show compassion for others.

All compassion starts with acceptance; acceptance of self and then acceptance of others. It is only after traveling through the gateway of acceptance that we can embark upon the road of change toward a better world—starting with ourselves.

SELF-COMPASSION EXERCISE

Cultivating compassion for yourself is a gradual process; something we need to work on a little bit each day. I find that affirmations can be a very powerful way to achieve this. Each morning after you wake, look at yourself in the mirror and recite a series of positive affirmations. I have a ritual like this I go through every morning and, from my experience, the best way to go about it is to list a number of your own attributes that you are grateful for:

I am grateful for being . . .
I am grateful for being . . .
I am grateful for being . . .

Then go on to list a series of roles you play in life that that you are good at, e.g. I am grateful for being a good father.

I am grateful for being a . . .
I am grateful for being a . . .
I am grateful for being a . . .

> Then end with a simple statement:
>
> *I am grateful for a Universe that is grateful for me.*

Friends and supporters of Obama often complained that he lacked an overarching vision. He had not clearly articulated a mission statement that spelled out his governing philosophy and brought together the different strands and achievements in his administration. No one doubted that he was smart or that he was capable, but what was his North Star?

Such longstanding gripes had been lurking in the background for some time. As the election cycle began revving up again in Spring 2011, the gripes started to seep into the foreground. How was he going to position himself against the Republicans? This came to a head on perhaps the most pressing question of the time: How to manage the government's budget deficit. The Republicans had laid down the gauntlet with a bold plan to cut the deficit, but it meant slashing the budget so harshly that the very fabric of society would be transformed. Longstanding entitlements like Medicare, Medicaid and Social Security would be diminished or even ended, while at the same time, tax cuts would be offered to the highest earners.

Obama, however, had yet to present a plan and the media chastised him daily for this. He bided his time. Then, on April 13th, in a lecture to George Washington University, he was ready to put his cards on the table. Where budget priorities were concerned, one word was going to be key: compassion.

"Each one of us deserves some basic measure of security and dignity. We recognize that no matter how responsibly we live our lives, hard times or bad luck, a crippling illness or a layoff may strike any one of us. 'There but for the grace of God go I,' we say to ourselves. And so we contribute to programs like Medicare and Social Security, which guarantee us healthcare and a measure of basic income after a lifetime of hard work; unemployment insurance, which protects us against unexpected job loss; and Medicaid, which provides care for millions of seniors in nursing homes, poor children, those with disabilities. We're a better country because of these commitments. I'll go further. We would not be a great country without those commitments."

Such a compassionate society, he believed, was not compatible with the vision put forward by the current Republican plan. "It's a vision that says up to 50 million Americans have to lose their health insurance in order for us to reduce the deficit. Who are these 50 million Americans? Many are somebody's grandparents—maybe one of yours—who wouldn't be able to afford nursing home care without Medicaid. Many are poor children. Some are middle-class families who have children with autism or Down's Syndrome. Some of these kids with disabilities are—the disabilities are so severe that they require 24-hour care. These are the Americans we'd be telling to fend for themselves."

This was not the America he knew, he declared. "The America I know is generous and compassionate. It's a land of opportunity and optimism. Yes, we take responsibility for ourselves, but we also take responsibility for each other; for the country we want and the future that we share. We're a nation that built a railroad across a continent and brought light to communities shrouded in darkness. We sent a generation to college on the GI Bill and we saved millions of seniors from poverty with Social Security and Medicare."

Compassion is at the core of America, indeed it is at the core of any civilized society, and this was Obama's vision. "We believe that in order to preserve our own freedoms and pursue our own happiness, we can't just think about ourselves. We have to think about the country that made these liberties possible. We have to think about our fellow citizens with whom we share a community . . . This sense of responsibility—to each other and to our country—this isn't a partisan feeling. It isn't a Democratic or a Republican idea. It's patriotism."

A clarion call had been sounded and the battle lines drawn for the fight ahead: A fight that would wage for years—first over the budget and then the election itself.

The next day, the airwaves across much of the media were filled with praise. A *New York Times* editorial declared Obama "reinvigorated" and the Pulitzer Prize-winning *Washington Post* columnist Eugene Robinson distilled the moment with characteristic clarity: "How selfish are we, really? How selfless? To what extent does this churchgoing nation take the biblical instruction to 'love thy neighbor' seriously? These are the kinds of basic choices we face. Obama's [plan] appeals to the better angels of our nature."

LESSON

MIRROR RESPECT

The launch of Obama's campaign for president rested initially on the shoulders of one man; Paul Tewes. He was the key man on the ground in Iowa. What he didn't know about the state and its Democratic electorate wasn't worth knowing, and so an early imperative for Obama's campaign was to forge a relationship between the candidate and Tewes.

Tewes had a distinct style of working that involved empowering each and every member of his team by giving them ever-greater responsibilities. This way, he was able to build formidable networks of organizers, all of whom professed a deep loyalty to the man who led them. This was exactly Obama's style too and so it was no surprise when the two men gelled from day one. As Richard Wolffe describes in his book *Renegade:* "For Tewes it was a perfect fit to work with a candidate who was a community organizer who wanted his staff and volunteers to feel empowered. Fieldwork was no longer the obscure, overlooked corner of a presidential campaign but the organizing principle behind it."

Obama made it his business to talk to workers in the field on a daily basis but he never gave them the impression that he wanted to micro-manage. He trusted them, and he wanted them to know that all the time. Wolffe tells us, "For the first few months when he visited Iowa, Obama would hear the latest numbers and news from Tewes. Then one day he listened patiently, before signaling that he didn't need them to justify their work. 'You know I trust you,' the candidate told Tewes. 'You guys know what you're doing. Keep doing what you're doing'"

The growing respect he possessed for the people working for him was a cornerstone of the campaign—the secret ingredient upon which layer after layer of support was built. Obama's press secretary at the time, Tommy Vietor, described the synergy that was evolving between Obama and Tewes. "Paul and Barack meshed so well in philosophy because Paul's whole worldview was empowering the lowest person on the totem pole. At Barack's events he'd have the organizers on stage with him. It would make us cry seeing these kids on stage."

The respect that grew was, of course, mutual. By the end of the Iowa primary campaign Obama had recruited an organization of some 10,000 volunteers in the state with 159 organizers. They made 8,279 calls in one day alone and targeted knocking on a total of 363,000 doors, despite the fact that only 125,000 Democrats had voted in Iowa in total in the last primary. Their targets were ambitious, but the organization they built was easily a match.

As January 2008 arrived, and caucus day came into sight, Obama took a final opportunity to express the gratitude and respect he felt for those who had come out for him during a speech in Theodore Roosevelt High School in Des Moines. "As I've traveled around the state in the last ten months I have been so inspired by the young people who have been organizing for us in counties across the state. They have put their heart and soul into this campaign, they have believed when others did not believe. I am so proud of what they have accomplished so far . . . This is the team that's put this all together . . . That's a good-looking bunch too isn't it? They're like a Benetton ad. You remember those?"

The day came and anxieties rose. The media couldn't help but notice, early on, that turnout had hit unprecedented levels. One of the campaigns must have pulled off something extraordinary. As voting began, it became clear whose campaign that was.

The results rolled in and started to paint a picture that was, only recently, considered unthinkable; not only had Obama beaten the formerly "inevitable" nominee, Hillary Clinton, but he had managed to push her into third place.

Tewes walked into the campaign office and watched the young staffers spraying champagne over each other. His elation rendered him virtually mute. He walked to a reception of big donors, saw his boss, and hugged him for the first time.

"We made history." Tewes began tearing up.

"Yes, we did," said Obama.

Compassion, as discussed in the previous lesson, is at our core. It is our foundation. A key ingredient of compassion is respect. Without respect, compassion is merely pity.

True respect is also a mutual tendency. It is hard to respect someone who does not feel the same for you and vice-versa. The most constructive relationships, whether personal, societal or professional, tend to be relationships of mutual respect. When we relate to other people it is a bit like two spoons facing each other. You see yourself in them and they see themselves in you. As a result, people who carry around a good dose of self-respect often find themselves experiencing such respect for others; self-respect tends to evoke the same in the other person, forming a mutually respectful virtuous cycle.

True respect is not an idealization or exaggeration of someone's worth, but a genuine appreciation of their value in a way that does not preclude their inevitable failings in some areas. To be truly respectful, you also need to be grounded and compassionate. Without compassion there can be no real respect, and without respect, there can be no real compassion.

Exuding compassion and respect will bring the same qualities back to you. Obama's entire campaign was built upon multiple layers of respect; projected by him towards his supporters, and then mirrored back to him by them.

When the opposite happens in a campaign it is often noticeable: A candidate starts to take his staff or voters for granted, but the electoral reaction in such cases can be swift and unforgiving.

His attitude of respect for those around and supporting him was a vital factor in generating the wave that carried Obama to the White House. And once he got there, he continued to demonstrate it to an extent that it even made those advisors closest to him more than a little bit uncomfortable on occasion.

———

Even before winning the election Obama had a vision of bringing the people he most respected into his administration. This would not necessarily be the people he agreed with the most. His model was Lincoln, about whose administration he learned from Doris Kearns Goodwin's award winning book *Team of Rivals*. One aide observed, "He talks about it all the time." In an interview with *Time* magazine's Joe Klein in the summer of '09, Obama began sketching out his ideas. Klein wrote: "He is particularly intrigued by the notion that Lincoln assembled all the Republicans who had run against him for president in his war cabinet, some of whom disagreed with him vehemently and persistently. 'The lesson is to not let your ego or grudges get in the way of hiring absolutely the best people,' Obama told me. 'I don't think the American people are fundamentally ideological. They're pragmatic . . . and so I have an interest in casting a wide net, seeking out people with a wide range of expertise, including Republicans,' for the highest positions in his government . . . I really admire the way the elder Bush negotiated the end of the Cold War—with discipline, tough diplomacy and restraint . . . and I'd be very interested in having those sorts of Republicans in my Administration, especially people who can expedite a responsible and orderly conclusion to the Iraq war—and who know how to keep the hammer down on al-Qaeda.'"

He resolved to draw people into a circle of mutual respect; one in which people did not necessarily agree with everything the others said, but respected one another enough to give each other a fair hearing and so reach an evolving consensus. The extent to which his thinking had advanced in this direction, however, would come as a bit of a shock to his most senior campaign advisors as the election drew to a close and the responsibilities of the presidency appeared on the horizon.

Lists of potential candidates for key cabinet posts started to be drawn up in the autumn. Most of the names for most of the posts were fairly predictable but for one of the most senior posts—Secretary of State—Obama wanted to make sure a name that no one predicted was firmly on his list; Hillary Clinton. Valerie Jarrett had to ask the question, "Are you serious about Senator Clinton?" Obama responded emphatically: "Yes I am." In their seminal behind-the-scenes account of the campaign *Game Change,* Mark Halperin and John Heilemann describe how the team reacted to this notion internally:

"Obama's campaign brain trust was resistant to the idea. The suits were skeptical that Hillary would be, could be, a loyal team player. The arguments against her varied among them but all were forcefully and fully aired. She would pursue her own agenda. She would undermine Obama's. She would be a constant headache. She would come attached to her globe-trotting, buckraking, headline-making husband, whose antics were the very antithesis of the no-drama-Obama way of doing business . . .

"Obama listened to the objections and more or less dismissed them . . . More than once, he calmly reassured Jarrett, 'She's going to be really good at this job.'"

He had watched her from close quarters during the election campaign and, though they were opponents—sometimes bitterly so—the more he observed her, the more he respected her. Halperin and Heilemann go on: "His praise for Clinton was effusive. She's smart, she's capable, she's tough, she's disciplined, Obama said again and again. She wouldn't have to be taught or have her hand held. She wouldn't have to earn her place on the world stage; she already had global stature. She pays attention to nuance, Obama told Jarrett, and that's what I want in a Secretary of State, because the stakes are so high. I can't have somebody who would put us in peril with one errant sentence."

Hillary's immediate reaction, when the rumors reached her ears, was one of suspicion. She assumed it was part of some grand game the Obama camp continued to play for their political advantage. Nevertheless she flew to Chicago at the request of the President-elect, only to be told directly by him that he was deadly serious. He described the relationship he envisioned; one in which there would be no overlap between their two roles. She would have autonomy and freedom within the framework of a global vision, which he knew they shared.

Halperin and Heilemann reveal, however, that "Hillary's head, when she flew out of Chicago, was in a different place. I'm not taking this job, she thought. And I'm not going to let anyone talk me into it—anyone . . . She had less than zero interest in working for Obama—for doing anything other than going back to the Senate, licking her wounds, and putting her energies into paying down her multimillion-dollar debt. She was looking forward to reclaiming some semblance of the life she'd had before the campaign. Going to the theatre. Dining out. Spending time with Chelsea. She was sixty-one years old and staring down the likelihood that she would never be president. And she was tired—oh, so tired."

Yet, at the same time, "Hillary felt the call of patriotism and the call of duty. She believed that when a president asked a person to serve, there was an imperative to say yes. And yet after five days of tumultuous to-ing and fro-ing she decided to decline Obama's offer. Her reasons were many and, to her, dispositive. Secretary of State, of all jobs, seemed designed to turn her life upside down in myriad ways—in particular, the constant travel and omnivorous jet lag."

Game Change goes on to describe how, at 1 AM on November 20th, Clinton finally managed to speak to Obama on the phone after trying to reach him all day. Her long rehearsed rejection came rolling out. "'It's not going to work,' an anguished Hillary told him. 'I can't do it. It was a long, hard campaign and I'm exhausted. I have this debt to pay down and I can't do that as Secretary of State. I'm tired of being punched around. I feel like a piñata. I want to go home. I've had enough of this. You don't want me. You don't want all these stories about you and me. You don't want the whole circus. It's not good for you, and it's not good for me. I can't do this.'"

'Hillary, look, you're exactly right,' Obama said. 'Those are all real concerns, they're all real problems, and it's fair and legitimate for you to raise them. And the truth is, there's really nothing I can do about them. But the thing is, the economy is a much bigger mess than we ever imagined it would be, and I'm gonna be focused on that for the next two years. So I need someone as big as you to do this job. I need someone I don't need to worry about. I need someone I can trust implicitly and you're that person . . . '"

Obama's tacit admission was revealing. As a public figure and a private man, his signal characteristics were supreme self-confidence and self-reliance. He needed no one, was better and smarter, cooler and more composed than anyone around him. But here he was conceding to Clinton that her help was crucial to the success of his presidency. For the first time, after all the bitterness and resentment that had passed between them as combatants, they had suddenly metamorphosed into different creatures with each other—human beings."

The next morning Jarrett inquired, first thing, how it went. He told her Hillary had said no, but she agreed to sleep on it and call him back again in the morning. A smile remained fixed to his face, however. He knew her well already. "She's going to do it."

Fast forward a couple of months into his presidency and the evidently synergistic relationship between President and Secretary of State was already winning rave reviews around the globe. Even Clinton's former critics in team Obama had to admit that she had gelled better than they ever expected with the boss. "They both worked really hard at it." Remarked a senior official. "There's a natural affinity and respect that ironically grew out of being opponents. You get to know someone really well after all that."

During my nearly two decades work in psychiatry I have worked with dozens of different mental health teams. Some of them were based in the community and some were hospital wards. Often, particularly in the hospital environment, where I work at present, the working relationship is very close and sometimes tense. I work as an attending psychiatrist (or attending consultant in the UK) to the team, which means that I take on the ultimate clinical responsibility as the chief clinician, so my role is one of leadership. In the past, management used to parachute me in to teams that were in someway considered problematic or dysfunctional to help turn them around. Each time this happened I went through a similar process. I would start just by observing how they work, staying in the background as much as possible. Almost invariably I started to notice a genuinely high degree of competence in much of the team.

As I started building a working relationship with the team I was then able to do so in an atmosphere of deep respect. This then percolated through to every team member, who then felt valued, raised their game, and started to complement each other's skills as a result. The atmosphere of mutual respect then spread to the relationship with our clients and, consequently, outcomes started to improve noticeably. The teams I have worked with have usually gone on to become very successful in what they do—and that is the challenging business of treating people with often very severe mental illnesses. And in each case it turned out that the ingredients for their success always existed within them in the first place.

Though I write this down as if it were a process, the truth is that it all goes on pretty much unconsciously when I am doing it, a bit like driving a car. I quickly get to the point where I am developing escalating levels of respect for the people I am working with—and for good reason—and this then feeds back to me too. The respect I gain from each job bolsters my own self-respect, which then enables me to utilize it when I start working with the next team. In other words, it all starts with the respect I have for myself.

My own self-respect is of course, like anyone else's, never perfect. As a result neither are the teams I work with and so there is always room for improvement and, again, that is always about self-improvement before team improvement.

I have seen other very good leaders work this way as well. In fact, most of the managers and directors in the organizations I work for have shown great respect to me too and this is often what fuels me to cascade it down to my own team. Mutual respect is a fundamental ingredient in the management of any team or organization; and as with every ingredient to success, it starts within.

Being able to respect yourself means you are fundamentally able to trust yourself. This means that you have a deep knowing inside that whatever happens, whatever mistakes, wrong turns or misjudgments you might make along the way, you will generally be able to get to where you want to go and achieve what you set out to do, or at least a result you're happy with. Trusting yourself—flaws and all—in this way is a form of liberation. And this will enable you to liberate others as well, for the attitude you present to others will generally be one of trust in them too. By showing others you trust them, wherever it is reasonable to do so, you will be liberating them to trust themselves. The ultimate consequence of respecting someone in this way is a facilitation of their autonomy. In other words, you give them the ultimate gift of independence.

The best way to respect someone, then, is to nurture and honor their capacity for autonomy. That might need time and facilitation, but it should always be the goal. That is how change is created for the better.

And you can practice the art of giving out this respect starting any minute of any day. You can start right now.

This form of liberation through respect is not only central to the way Obama deals with other people in his team; it is also fundamental to the way in which he handles foreign policy and, as the leader of the free world, deals with other nations too.

————

Since before the invasion of Iraq, a transfer of sovereignty back to Iraq itself was always the ultimate objective. This was a lot more difficult to achieve in practice than in theory, however. Indeed, more than five years after the initial invasion, it remained a relatively remote prospect. The problem lay, of course, in the fact that Iraq had been a country with little infrastructure outside the direct jurisdiction of the regime that had just been toppled. The entire state apparatus had to be rebuilt from scratch. This would take time effort and determination, but meanwhile the nation continued to remain dependent on US aid and administration.

Such situations become particularly difficult when a culture of dependency sets in and the very support itself becomes an obstacle to independence. That is the scenario that the Obama administration inherited when it came to office. Obama had made a commitment, however, to withdraw all combat troops from Iraq within 16 months of taking office and the wider objective was to wean Iraq off American dependence, in all its forms, as well. "We were determined to take them seriously about restoration of sovereignty," said one senior official. "We needed to cut the umbilical cord; otherwise you have a never-ending dependency."

Though for Obama this was a key priority, he also arrived to a vast inbox of competing priorities including an economy in deep recession and another war in Afghanistan, fast slipping out of control. In the transition phase he had relied on Vice President Joe Biden to make visits to the region and feedback to him about the status on the ground. Soon after reaching office, he called Biden in for a meeting.

"Joe, I think it would be great if you take this on. This needs to have sustained focus from the White House. You're the guy to do it. You spent more time in Iraq than anyone. You know the players. You just do Iraq."

Biden was taken aback. "Whoa, Mr. President . . . Sign me up."

It was a sign to the Vice President, early in their working relationship, of the deep respect and high esteem in which the President held him. He set about justifying that straight away, and he would do it by facilitating the autonomy of the Iraqi government by demonstrating the same respect to them.

Biden's weekly schedule centered heavily around Iraq from then on, but his intention was always to be a relatively quiet background presence while allowing—and trusting—them to run their own elections and form their own government. The philosophy was outlined by Tony Blinken, his national security advisor. "It was important not to be overly heavy-handed, but for us to weigh in quietly when it looked like things were going off the rails. Compare that to the much more blatant Iranian efforts. Iraqis don't want other countries to decide their future for them."

Biden's pivotal role in helping Iraqi leaders navigate their way to a sovereign stable state, and the way he went about it, was documented by Richard Wolffe in *Revival*: "Biden's strength was his personality and his political longevity. He could connect with Iraqi politicians as someone who has experienced the highs and lows of life, including the loss of the Democratic primaries to Barack Obama. 'He can get on the phone and really engage them as someone who has been through elections and understands the political pressures on politicians themselves. He can talk to them in a way that military leaders and diplomats just can't get to,' said Biden's Chief of Staff, Ron Klain. 'Managing Iraq has largely been about managing this process of political reconciliation.'"

Again, the fostering of mutually respectful relationships— empathizing and understanding one another's viewpoints—was the bedrock of the strategy. And it all stemmed from the "team of rivals" approach Obama took to his officials at the very top of government in the first place. "In an Oval Office address marking the end of combat operations in Iraq at the end of August, Obama praised the troops and even President Bush," wrote Richard Wolffe. "There was no sense of triumph or even mission accomplished; only sacrifice, perseverance and responsibility. The irony was that the people he relied on the end the war were two former Democratic rivals in the 2008 campaign—Biden and Hillary Clinton—and his predecessor's Defense Secretary, Robert Gates."

MIRROR MEDITATION

Read these notes then close your eyes and take yourself gently through each step. Alternatively, you will find this guided meditation, for you to simultaneously listen to and practice, online at www.obamakarma.org/mirror.html:

- Sit or stand in a comfortable position. Keep your back straight and unsupported, so you're relaxed but upright.
- Start by taking a few deep breaths and feel your lungs fill with clean air on the in-breath, and empty completely on the out-breath.
- Gently close your eyes or, if you prefer, leave them open but focused only softly on what is before you.

- Now spend a moment listening to the sounds around you, around the room and outside it. The sound of stillness, motion, noise or what ever happens to be there.

- Now turn your focus within. You are a microcosm of the whole world. Using metaphor to experience your inner world, imagine yourself as the whole planet. Feel the energy flow around you—the different peoples, races, countries and continents—they are all a part of you.
- Your thoughts and feelings are as diverse as the people on the planet and you experience them chattering, traveling, doing, living.
- All is you and you are all.
- And the love and respect that flows from your heart, gently surrounds and lightly embraces it all.
- Observe the world, through yourself, in this gentle loving embrace.
- Sit with it. Treasure it. And just be, for a few minutes.

- After several minutes, gradually return to the broader awareness of the room around you; imagine its features before opening your eyes, looking around and giving yourself a few moments to reorient.

Try this whenever you can. Simply close your eyes, take a few deep breaths and reflect the beauty of the world within you.

THE RESPECT MIRROR EXERCISE

The way in which we respect others is a genuine reflection of the way in which we respect ourselves. The more self-respect we have, the more respect we are able to project onto the outside world. This means that by exploring the positive feelings we have towards other people, we can get a good idea of our own positive qualities.

For example, if we think of someone we particularly respect; whether that be someone close to us or a more remote role model, and list the attributes in them we admire the most, they should actually correspond pretty well with the positive traits that exist in ourselves already (only others are more easily able to see them than we are). This is a good way of getting to know and appreciate ourselves and our true nature more deeply.

You can try it any time just by filling in a simple form like this:

Name of person I admire:	His/her positive attributes:

Then cover over the first column, look at what you have written, and realize that these are actually your own attributes. If you think a little deeper, you will be able to start finding examples of each of them in your own character and life story.

GAIN STRENGTH FROM PAIN

"An educated fool!" That was the conclusion Congressman Bobby Rush reached about Barack Obama during Obama's first run for national office in 2000. Worse still, by the time the votes were counted on election night, it seemed that the voters of the 1st District in Illinois agreed with Rush. He beat Obama 2 to 1.

Rep. Rush had served four terms in the US Congress, he had a long history with voters, who knew him as a Baptist minister, a veteran of the civil rights battles of the '60s, and a founding member of the Illinois branch of the Black Panthers. In 1999, however, he ran for Mayor of Chicago and was trounced by Richard Daley. Suddenly he seemed vulnerable. After serving only a single term as state Senator, Obama, seen as a rising star by the local Democratic Party, made his move against Rush. Though he had, to date, only served a few years in the State Senate, the achievements he had notched up during that period had won him high praise from a variety of quarters. He had championed healthcare and campaign finance reform, brought the seemingly intractable debate over the state's death penalty to an amicable consensus conclusion, and fought to end the police practice of racial profiling.

Obama launched his campaign with gusto. Don Gonyea of NPR reported, "Obama went door to door, shaking hands and having countless conversations on front porches across the district. He talked of his record at the statehouse in Springfield over the previous three years." And when people raised the issue of his lack of experience, he pushed back hard. "I've represented afford-able housing organizations that build affordable housing, some-thing that's a major issue in the district," Obama said. "I've been a community organizer and helped design programs at the ground level." His experience was broader and deeper than just the po-litical.

Watching this young pretender fly made the older Rush's blood boil. He adjusted his campaign into attack mode and made a case to the voters that could be summed up in five words: "Obama's not one of us."

Some of Obama's own actions seemed to somehow feed in to that very narrative. When black students were expelled from a central Illinois school for two years over a fight, the Rev. Jesse Jackson stepped in to demand a lesser punishment. Rush and an-other congressional candidate stood squarely behind Jackson. Only after their endorsement, did Obama cautiously follow.

His relationship with voters appeared hampered by his profes-sorial style, as he pontificated on solutions to people's problems in the language of high policy and detailed manifestos. As Rush put it, "We're not impressed with these folks with these eastern elite degrees." A veteran of the civil rights campaign, Mark Allen, who also viewed Obama's 2000 congressional campaign from close quarters remembers the voters' reaction well: "You egotistical son of a gun, you sound like you're talking above people. Here comes the highfaluting guy, the Harvard guy."

Obama started responding to the criticism. The heat of the campaign began molding him as a candidate. Chicago City Council member Toni Preckwinkle, an early Obama supporter, said, "I think he took a hard look at himself . . . and became a much better campaigner, more at ease on the campaign trail."

But it wasn't enough. Rush's narrative seemed too powerful. Voters remained mindful of Obama's lack of experience as a public official, which made him appear too ambitious as a result. This, coupled with the tragic murder of Rush's son days before the poll and the public outpouring of sympathy that followed, meant that Obama's numbers tanked.

By the time of the election, Obama polled less than half of Rush's vote.

A rapidly ascending political career had suddenly come screeching to a halt. The golden boy of Chicago's Hyde Park became a loser for the first time; his trajectory stalled, seemingly for good.

He attended Al Gore's nominating convention later that year as the Democratic Party started to move into gear for what promised to be a nail biting national election. But, upon his arrival, Obama's credentials weren't accepted. He wasn't even allowed in. He returned home, dejected.

Many would have quit at that point. Indeed, Obama did consider it. He told NPR, "I had to really look into myself and say, why am I doing this? Is it to get attention or is it to help people?" A period of soul-searching ensued. He started to accept that it was "hubris on my part" to think he could oust an incumbent who had given voters no strong reason to be dissatisfied.

Acknowledging his pain and flaws, Obama started to survey the debris for gains. As it turned out, they weren't so hard to find. As Gonyea observed, "Even in losing, Obama gained plenty in losing to Rush. He vastly improved his name recognition. He made political friends and gained fundraising experience. And he ran a relatively positive campaign, emerging without having burned any political bridges."

He analyzed his campaigning style and how he connected with voters. "It was a learning process," said Mark Allen. "He recognized that and understood the criticism."

Through the wreckage of his defeat, Obama started to fashion a new trajectory for himself. Within four years he was back at the Democratic National Convention, this time for John Kerry, and this time Obama was a candidate for the U.S. Senate. The speech he gave propelled him to international celebrity status overnight, and a little over four years later he was President of the United States.

————

It was written thousands of years ago but no one is quite sure by whom. Some say it was a letter from Aristotle to Alexander the Great. Who ever wrote it, it eventually came to be known as The Emerald Tablet.

It was translated into dozens of languages and the first Latin translation in 1140 heralded it The Secret of Secrets. Scholars, scientists and philosophers through the ages—from Newton to the makers of the recent film "The Secret"—have been fascinated by its contents, yet its central message is very simple:

"That which is below is like that which is above, and that which is above is like that which is below."

To me, there is indeed a great truth here; namely that there is much we can learn about ourselves and our inner world by exploring the universe on a larger scale. We are all microcosms of the universe. For this reason, parallels between the laws of physics in the outer world, and the laws of psychology in the inner world, have always appeared to resonate.

One such example arose with the launch of the Hubble Space Telescope in 1990. Through it we were suddenly able to explore the galaxies around us in greater detail than ever before. An early finding in one of our neighboring galaxies startled physicists. Sitting right in the center of that galaxy they found a black hole. This was a shock. No one expected it. All the solar systems of that galaxy appeared to be circling this black hole. Researchers looking at another nearby galaxy also stumbled on a black hole in that one too. It sat right in the center—just like the other one. Pretty soon the race of exploration was on and galaxy after galaxy turned out to have a black hole in the center. This led the scientific community in only one direction. What about our own galaxy? All eyes turned to the center of our own galaxy, the Milky Way, and sure enough, sitting right there in the center was a black hole.

Like the others, it lies dormant, but it was undoubtedly once active. An avalanche of measurements followed as scientists busily tried to figure out what this was all about. What they then found was that there was a relationship between the radius of any galaxy and the size of the black hole that sits within it. This, they surmised, could only mean one thing; namely that the galaxy and the black hole that sits within it were somehow related to each other. The combination couldn't be based on a random chance of a black hole somehow finding its way into the center of a random galaxy. They were profoundly connected to one another in some way.

Further digging, analyzing, math and extrapolation led to a theory that is now the accepted story of how galaxies themselves were created. It starts with a star at the end of its life. As it dies it collapses in on itself and forms a black hole. The black hole then unleashes its destructive force on the Universe and begins to suck in all the matter around it. As matter pours in, it begins to swirl around it like water around a drain. Through this swirling process debris starts to clump together. These clumps of debris then grow and start to develop their own gravitational force, which then enables each of them to suck in further debris, grow larger and eventually form stars.

In other words the very act of destruction unleashed by the black hole is itself the driving force behind the creation of stars themselves. It is the negative force that creates the positive. Creation and destruction are opposite sides of the same coin. You cannot have one without the other. This is a process that is mirrored at all levels of the Universe.

Another example, closer to home, is forest fires. Such fires are, of course, common in many parts of the world. You have probably heard a lot about the danger and destruction wrought upon landscapes by such events every summer. What you may not have heard, however, is that sometimes—so long as these fires are not encroaching on populated areas—they are left to continue burning. Why? Because it has a positive effect too. Several forms of tree, when they burn, release pods into the air, which contain seeds. These seeds then fall and are buried into the ground during a fire. In the weeks, months and years after the fire, a new, fresh and vital forest then grows from these very seeds. In fact, there are several species of tree that cannot reproduce without the aid of fire. So here again, an act of destruction has been responsible for a new creation; indeed, it is sometimes necessary for new creation to occur!

The fact is that if it wasn't for negative energy in the Universe there would be no positive. If not for dark, there would be no light, you cannot have a peak without a valley or a day without night, or white without black or high without low. They are interdependent and, not only that, it is usually the negative force that is the creative.

So much of the art and literature we see around us is a product of the pain contained within the artists mind. Whether it's through heartbreak or mental illness, the concept of a tortured artist is common to all cultures. Negativity is a precursor to creativity, pain is a precursor to pleasure, and failure is a precursor to success.

So the dark shades contained within are not to be shunned or ignored. Our disappointments, anguish, fears, losses, sadness and anger is not to be hidden away or "fixed" out of existence, nor is it to be discharged into the world outside. It is to be honored. It is not only inevitable but it is necessary for light to exist too.

The key to success in life is not to deny the negatives, but to harness them. It's not just that every cloud has a silver lining. It is that every cloud *is* a silver lining.

Through my journey in the world of psychology and psychiatry I have explored and studied many forms of treatment and therapy. After a decade and a half of practice, I noticed a particular school of psychotherapy was gaining increasing prominence. It seemed to be based on a very rigorous theoretical framework and was backed up by some increasingly robust research data. Not only that, but as a mindfulness-based therapy, I found that it also emphasized the very elements of personal development I had found of most value in my own personal and professional life. Its name is Acceptance and Commitment Therapy (ACT; pronounced as if it were a word rather than an acronym). One of ACT's seminal texts is a book called *Get Out Of Your Mind and Into Your Life* by Steven Hayes and Spencer Smith, and in it they talk of the importance of willingness to experience life to the fullest, warts and all. It's a very interesting passage, and here's how they define what willingness means:

WILLINGNESS IS:

- Holding your pain as you would a delicate flower in your hand
- Embracing your pain as you would embrace a crying child
- Sitting with your pain the way you would sit with a person who has a serious illness
- Looking at your pain the way you would look at an incredible painting
- Walking with your pain the way you would walk while carrying a sobbing infant
- Honoring your pain the way you would honor a friend by listening
- Inhaling your pain the way you would take a deep breath
- Abandoning the war with your pain like a soldier who puts down his weapons to walk home
- Getting with your pain like drinking a glass of pure water
- Carrying your pain the way you carry a picture in your wallet

WILLINGNESS IS NOT:

- Resisting your pain
- Ignoring your pain
- Forgetting your pain
- Buying your pain
- Doing what your pain says
- Not doing what your pain says
- Believing your pain
- Not believing your pain

How we handle our pain determines, as much as anything else, who we are and what we make of life. Obama learned this lesson early and continues, like many of us, to learned it over and over again each day, not least during the single biggest ordeal of his life to date up to 2007; running for the Presidency of the United States.

———

Their strategy was simple. Win Iowa, then New Hampshire. Game over. They would become unassailable. The Obama campaign spent a whole year in Iowa building their campaign and in the end they pulled off the surprise upset they had been dreaming of. In Iowa the Clinton juggernaut had been knocked off track in a way that no one could have predicted just a few weeks earlier. For David Plouffe, the feeling was sweet. The endgame was in sight. The campaign was running perfectly to plan.

"This, I thought, had to be one of the best feelings in American politics—to be pulling up to the Des Moines airport, your charter waiting, taking off into the early morning skies as the winner of the Iowa caucuses, heading to New Hampshire with the momentum at your back.

"As we pulled up, though, we had a bit of a surprise: we had to wait before proceeding to the tarmac because the Clinton plane was taking off. As we cooled our heels I had a delicious thought: this will be the last time she's ever in front of us again . . .

"As we reached cruising altitude I settled back into my seat. 'Hope they enjoy that charter up ahead of us. She could be flying commercial sooner than she thinks.'"

The few days between the Iowa and New Hampshire elections went by like a daze. They were all on a high, surrounded by an expectant media ready to declare the Clinton candidacy dead and the Obama team as the giant slayers.

"And then suddenly we were falling." Plouffe recalls. As polling results started filtering in an assured win started to look more and more shaky. Then, like melting ice cream, their victory morphed into defeat. The senior campaign team watched the exit polls on election night transfixed. Richard Wolffe recounts in *Revival*:

> "They waited for a little data to confirm their worse fears, then Axelrod, David Plouffe and Robert Gibbs took the long walk to the elevator and to Obama's suite. The news was as stunning as it was dismal. The polls were wildly wrong and so was their strategy. There was no tidal wave. Iowa's momentum had rippled and faded . . .
>
> "Obama's closest aides walked down the hotel hallway dreading every step, but they wanted to deliver the news themselves. They knocked on the door and the candidate answered. Obama was immediately struck by the morose look on the faces of all three aides as they stood in the hallway. 'I think we may not have made it,' Axelrod told him. 'We're going to be a couple of points short.'
>
> " . . . Obama shook his head and leaned back against the wall. 'This thing is going to go on for a while isn't it?' he said with a wry smile."

All sorts of questions were swimming around in the team's minds. How could this have happened? In the closing hours every single uncommitted voter must have gone Clinton's way. They tried desperately to make sense of it.

Later that night, however, after some deeper pondering, Obama caught up with the rest to give his wider verdict. "I actually think this is for the best," he said. "Sure if we had won New Hampshire, we'd be in the driver's seat. But I'd be like a comet streaking across the sky. White hot. And comets eventually burn up. Now people can see how I deal with adversity, whether we can bounce back . . . They want me to earn this. They don't want it to be easy for someone like me and it probably shouldn't be."

The candidate's reaction blew his team away. Wolffe describes how, "Plouffe was even more stunned walking back than he was walking there. 'This guy really has what it takes to be President,' he thought to himself. 'There's not a lot of people who would react like that.'"

Soon after, Obama was preparing for his concession speech. Around him were elected New Hampshire officials who had staked their reputation on supporting Obama. Absorbing their pained expressions in one corner of the room was Valerie Jarrett. She started to cry. Obama spotted her and walked over. He placed a hand on her shoulder.

"Are you OK?"

His concern for her feelings, amidst all that was going on, took her aback. "I'm OK if you're OK." She said.

"I'm fine," he replied. "This is a test. Who said it would be easy? It will make us stronger. This is going to be alright, you'll see."

———

Every single one of us has experienced moments of challenge, hardship, loss or failure in one form or another. Yet, in every such case, if we really think about it, there was usually a gain, opportunity or positive series of events that flowed from it. In some way we always grew. We often discount or fail to remember this because the pain is often the most powerful memory. But gaining an appreciation of the way in which light has so often followed dark during the course of our lives, can be very strengthening. The next exercise is designed as a way of cultivating this.

GAIN FROM PAIN EXERCISE

In the left hand column list some of the sad moments or set-backs in your life. This could be anything from a disappointing failure to a deeply felt bereavement. These can be times of great pain and anguish and they need and deserve to be honored. One way of doing this—if you can—is to think back to them, contemplate them for a few moments, and then focus on what followed as a result. You will find that for each negative event that occurred, unbeknownst to you at the time, subsequently, sometime in the future, something positive transpired as a result. Whether it was something you gained internally or externally, you will always have gained something. Complete this chart and you will know what I mean. Then spend a few minutes pondering it. It's a very grounding exercise.

Negative Events:	Positives that followed:

On a wider scale, we all start with an original bedrock of suffering that stems from our childhoods. No process of learning and growing can avoid pain and so no childhood can

ever be free from it. This in turn fuels much of our productiv-
ity and drive in later life.

For some, this process is more intense than others, and
here again, Obama's own example is a good illustration.

Growing up without his father left the young Barack Obama
deprived in a way that was painful, even more deeply than it is for
most children brought up by a single parent. Neither his mother
nor any of the family who raised him could ever fill the African
void in his identity. There was a whole part of his life, his existence that he was not in touch with and he was reminded of it
every time he looked in the mirror. On the one occasion in which
they actually met and spent time together when he was 10, the
young Barack tried hard to grow close to and form a bond with
his father.

"For brief spells in the day I will lie beside him, the two of us
alone in the apartment sublet from a retired old woman whose
name I forget, the place full of quilts and dollies and knitted seat
covers, and I read my book while he reads his. He remains opaque
to me, a present mass; when I mimic his gestures or turns of
phrase, I know neither their origins nor their consequences, can't
see how they play out over time. But I grow accustomed to his
company."

But it wasn't to last. "Two weeks later he was gone. In that
time we stand together in front of the Christmas tree and pose for
pictures, the only ones I have of us together, me holding an orange
basketball, his gift to me, him showing off the tie I've brought
him."

The photo has made it through the corridors of time to the
present day, where it is now in public circulation for all to see.

And in that time the journey of soul-searching Obama undertook has been a long and painful one.

Not long after his father returned to Africa, his mother was planning to move back to Indonesia for her work. She suggested he go with her but his answer was immediately no. He felt that America was his home. "I wearied of being new all over again." And besides, he had an agreement with his grandparents that he could stay if he so chose. "The arrangement suited my purpose," he explained in *Dreams From My Father*. It was, "a purpose that I could barely articulate to myself, much less to them. Away from my mother, away from my grandparents, I was engaged in a fitful interior struggle. I was trying to raise myself to be a black man in America, and beyond the given of my appearance, no one around me seemed to know exactly what that meant."

This was a struggle that carried on right through his college years and it was often quickly evident to people he met, such as a fellow black student named Regina, one of the first people he befriended on campus. He recalls when they first met, "We ended up spending the afternoon together, talking and drinking coffee. She told me about her childhood in Chicago, the absent father and struggling mother, the South Side six-flat that never seemed warm enough in winter and got so hot in the summer that people went out by the lake to sleep. She told me about the neighbors in her block, about walking past the taverns and pool halls on their way to church on Sunday. She told me about evenings in the kitchen with uncles and cousins and grandparents, the stew of voices bubbling up in laughter. Her voice evoked a vision of black life in all its possibility, a vision that filled me with a longing—a longing for place, and a fixed and definite history. As we were getting up to leave, I told Regina I envied her.

"'For what?'

"'I don't know. For your memories, I guess.'"

It was only years after his father's death that his journey of discovery took the next step. He decided to finally make good on the promise he had made to himself long ago and travel to Africa to meet his father's side of his family. He met cousins, half-siblings, aunts and uncles and one day was finally taken to his grandmother in the village.

There he learned of his forefathers. She told him about his grandfather who was a trailblazer in his own way. He left the village and traveled for days on foot to reach Nairobi where he started to work for the white British establishment who formed the ruling class back in colonial days. He earned a reputation as a tough, smart and trustworthy worker and stood out from, indeed offended, everyone else in the village when he returned home wearing only western clothes. They had never seen anything like that before. Over time, he returned with decreasing frequency as he found himself fitting in less and less with the folks back home. Back in the city he had to "reinvent himself in this arid, solitary place. Through force of will, he will create a life out of the scraps of an unknown world, and the memories of a world rendered obsolete."

Obama's father took the frontier and defiance to a new level, traveling to America and marrying an American woman against the wishes of his own family who feared how he might be received in white circles. His journey wasn't an easy one either. Obama found pages of letters in his grandmother's house from his father to countless universities in America. His father started out as a clerk in a firm with little education but he was spotted by some friendly Americans who offered to provide a reference for him if he ever wanted to study in the U.S. So, in between work, he started to fill out applications. The visiting young Obama imagined the scene.

"He, too, will have to invent himself. His boss is out of the office; he sets the forms aside and from an old file cabinet pulls out a list of addresses. He yanks the typewriter toward him and begins to type, letter after letter after letter, typing the envelopes, sealing the letters like messages in bottles that will drop through a post office slot into a vast ocean and perhaps allow him to escape."

Picturing the seminal scenes in the lives of his forefathers, Barack Obama II finally stepped out to face his past. There in the backyard of his grandmother's house were the graves of his father and grandfather.

"I went out to the backyard. Standing before the two graves I felt everything around me—the cornfields, the mango tree, the sky—closing in, until I was left with only a series of mental images, Granny's stories come to life . . .

"I dropped to the ground and swept my hand across the smooth yellow tile. Oh, father, I cried. There was no shame in your confusion. Just as there had been no shame in your father's before you. No shame in the fear, or in the fear of his father's before him . . .

"For a long time I sat between the graves and wept. When my tears were finally spent, I felt a calmness wash over me. I felt the circle finally close. I realized that who I was, what I cared about was no longer just a matter of intellect or obligation, no longer a construct of words. I saw that my life in America—the black life, the white life, the sense of abandonment I'd felt as a boy, the frustration and hope I'd witnessed in Chicago—all of it was connected with this small plot of earth an ocean away, connected by more than an accident of name or the color of my skin. The pain I felt was my father's pain . . . Their struggle was my birthright."

Obama came to realize that he was not alone in his struggle. It was the same struggle, a struggle for identity, for discovery and for a place in the world that his father and his father before him had endured. He embraced the suffering. He was no longer running from the pain. And through that realization he became liberated. His un-denied pain would guide him in his own unique way down his own unique path.

———

We all have pain to embrace in our lives. As outlined in previous chapters, it starts with the original suffering of existence—of needs wants and drives that can never entirely be fulfilled. Then there's the constant stream of thoughts and language, from which arises a vast terrain of fluctuating emotion within us throughout our waking lives.

We all have our own flavor of pain that reflects our own background and circumstances. My parents, for example, are from Bangladesh. It is one of the poorest countries in the world. Even though they were relatively well off—for that country's standards—the lack of security in their lives was almost unimaginable by Western standards. Despite its huge population (it is the most densely populated country on earth), as it sits on a broad stringy delta, every year in the summer rainy season, when the flood waters descend from the Himalayas, entire villages sink under the water. The poverty and crime that inevitably evolve from such an unstable environment ultimately affect society at every level. Though my parents' lives transformed dramatically when they immigrated to England, they still carry within them elements of that same pain and fear from their homeland. In addition, as part of the Indian subcontinent, the whole culture they came from has been influenced by British colonial rule, which, despite the undoubted technological and economic developments it brought with it, also denied the local population the right to self-government for hundreds of years. This cultivates a mindset of inferiority—or sometimes an overcompensating superiority—which still exists in many who experienced colonialism, often subconsciously, when comparing themselves to Europeans.

And although I was brought up from birth in the UK, hints of these ingredients exist within me too. They are my heritage. Sometimes when I meditate I touch them in the deepest recesses of my being, other times in my day-to-day life, I might notice them in the way I react to certain things. I see it in my sister too.

But all this pain has a positive side as well. It also fuels my drive for security, success and ever-deepening personal growth. And perhaps, without these drives I wouldn't be writing this book right now. And you wouldn't be reading it either. So you see, without the darkness there can be no light. We all possess within us the potential to add to the light in the universe, and that is because we all possess darkness and pain.

The problem often is, though, when we feel this pain we are frequently tempted to deal with it using the same reflex we use to deal with our external problems; namely, to "fix it," or make it go away. We are by nature a problem-solving species so we will put our brains to great and fruitful effect when dealing with problems in the outer world. We will find a way to remove obstacles or overcome hurdles in a series of very logical stages that deals with what is immediately before us one step at a time. The problem is that when it comes to the inner world, and the problem of emotional pain, it doesn't work. We can't just remove it like we can any other obstacle, nor can we side step or jump over it. But that doesn't stop us from trying.

We actually end up spending a lot of our lives exerting a great deal of effort into the process of resisting our inner pain. In the world of Acceptance and Commitment Therapy, this is known as experiential avoidance. But the avoidance itself is what then makes the pain even worse—pushing us to unhealthy levels of stress and/or mental illness. ACT has shown, through a strong body of research, that the very act of resisting our inner experiences actually exacerbates the pain itself. A quick example right now:

DON'T THINK OF PINK ELEPHANTS!

Oh dear, you just did. Of course you did, and that's because we can't just try and shut things out of our mind at will and, when we try it, we end up with more of what we were trying to avoid. The solution is actually counter to our usual intuition: It is to experience, or go into, that very thing we have been trying to avoid.

A metaphor often used in ACT is that of quicksand. If you are stuck in it, your natural reaction is to struggle to get out. The very act of struggling, however, leads to you gradually sinking deeper in. Your moving feet will bury you ever downward. Instead, if you try to lie into the quicksand and increase the amount of surface area contact you have with it, you will stop digging yourself in and, ultimately, be able to roll outwards.

It's the same with our emotional world. Hiding away or frantically struggling to dig ourselves out of it will never work. We need to embrace it. It's that old paradox again; it is only through acceptance that change becomes possible.

In practical terms, the way to harness these pools of emotional pain is to actually feel them within your body. Feeling it in this way is the middle ground between suppressing them—trying to ignore something you can't—and acting them out and inflicting them on the world around you. Neither of those two alternatives is desirable and, in their own way, they are both forms of avoidance. By feeling the pain and sitting with it, in time, you'll actually be able to channel it toward creative energy. That's the difference between channeling your pain and acting it out. The latter is instantaneous. You don't process the pain at all. It goes from entry to exit without passing "Go" in between. Channeling your emotional pain, on the other hand, means that you are allowing it to pass through you first and the more you do this, the more you are transforming it into a fuel that will ultimately propel you towards better things and help you live life the way you want. Your pain will then be working for you as opposed to against you, and that is because you have taken the time to befriend it.

These emotional pains are the batteries that fuel so much of what you achieve in life. They are at the core of the engine of human progress. There is not a single one of us who does not possess it within, in our own unique shape and form. That is why it needs to be embraced so that—like an egg about to hatch—it will release something beautiful.

The other benefit of feeling our pain in this way is that it will help us better connect with the rest of humankind because, in a broad sense, this is a shared human pain. Everyone has their own individual issues and experiences that have shaped their pain, of course, but the existence of pain is a universal phenomenon and so by connecting with it you are, at a very deep level, connecting with all others too.

Meditating on this can be extraordinarily powerful.

GOLDEN EGG MEDITATION

Read these notes then close your eyes and take yourself gently through each step. Alternatively, you will find this guided meditation, for you to simultaneously listen to and practice, online at www.obamakarma.org/egg.html:

- Sit or stand in a comfortable position. Keep your back straight and unsupported, so you're relaxed but upright.
- Start by taking a few deep breaths and feel your lungs fill with clean air on the in-breath, and empty completely on the out-breath.
- Gently close your eyes or, if you prefer, leave them open but focused only softly on what is before you.
- Now spend a moment listening to the sounds around you, around the room and outside it. The sound of stillness, motion, noise or what ever happens to be there.

- Start to feel inside your own body; the bands of light and dark, pleasure and pain, heaviness and lightness that are contained within you.
- Now, begin to focus your awareness on the areas of pain within you. Parts of you that feel heavier and sadder than others. There may be one, there may be many, they may be large or small.
- This is the pain of your humanity and the pain of your unique life story, from your childhood all the way to the present day. It has long been neglected. By staying with it, you honor it.
- These are your golden eggs. There is a golden child inside each golden egg who will grow with your attention and love to become towering parts of you.
- Now imagine tiny versions of yourself surrounding and hugging your golden eggs of pain. Deep and warm, long deserved hugs.
- As you spend a few moments now gently holding them inside you, know that this pain will bring to you your future happiness and peace.

- And it is this pain that links you with all of humanity.
- You are thankful for this pain. Sit with it for a few minutes.

- After several minutes, gradually return to the broader awareness of the room around you; imagine its features before opening your eyes, looking around and giving yourself a few moments to reorient.

Try this whenever you can. Simply close your eyes, take a few deep breaths and take some time to feel, appreciate and embrace your golden eggs of pain within.

STAY IN THE TENSION

(...AND DON'T LET THE ODDS GET YOU DOWN)

t was July 2006 and Obama was a freshman Senator. He was about as far down the pecking order as it was possible to be within the Senate, which meant he was essentially at the beck and call of his party's leadership. That's why, when the Senate Majority Leader, Senator Harry Reid, summoned Obama to his office, the immediate reaction was one of anxiety. "I wonder what we screwed up?" He remarked to his then press secretary, Robert Gibbs, as he walked out the door.

Reid was over twenty years Obama's senior and had been in the Senate almost a quarter century. The Senate's most powerful member sat across his desk from Obama and looked him up and down. Their relationship was formal and not particularly warm and, in keeping with this, Reid didn't beat around the bush.

"You're not going to go anyplace here . . . I know you don't like it, doing what you're doing." Having spent a political lifetime in the Senate, Reid knew who had the staying power and who was just passing through. As far as he was concerned, Obama was in the latter category. For his part, Obama wasn't sure where Reid was taking the conversation, and then suddenly it came. Reid made his point . . .

Obama left after only twenty minutes.

Gibbs looked on expectantly as soon as Obama returned. "So?" he waited for an answer, then tried again, "what did we fuck up?"

"Nothing," Obama replied. "Harry wants me to run for President."

"That whole meeting was about you running for President?"

"Yeah," Obama grinned. "He really wants me to run for President."

On the one hand, like everyone else, Obama thought the idea preposterous. How was a man not yet two years out of the Illinois statehouse supposed to beat the most powerful candidate for the presidential nomination in recent history? But, on the other hand, given recent encouragements from a variety of quarters, he had an obligation to at least genuinely consider it. Some ideas about how and why this might be possible began to grow in his head but the uncertainty raged as he called together his closest friends and advisors to seek their counsel.

David Plouffe recalls the meeting. "Barack did ask questions about the politics and, to a person, we all said that Hillary was an enormously strong front-runner. In fact, at this point, it was tough to see how she could lose . . . She was the eight-hundred-pound gorilla, with organizations in every state, 100 percent name recognition, and a fund-raising machine ready to be switched on at a moment's notice. We had none of this. Nothing, nada, zilch. Any political conversation about the 2008 primaries started and ended with Hillary Clinton."

And Plouffe didn't mince his words when it came to the impact on Obama's family life either. "As you make this decision, just think your 2007 and 2008 could be wonderful if you don't

run. You don't have reelection until 2010, you can take most week-
ends off, you can spend all the time with your family that you
want. You could have a wonderful period of time. The book is
selling well. But if you run, you'll never see your family, you'll be
under pressure the likes of which you can't imagine, and it will be
absolutely miserable from a personal standpoint."

Also in the room was Steve Hildebrand who had been running Democratic campaigns for years. He had taken Obama to a
couple of outings to test the waters in Iowa and was blown away
by the response. He was perhaps the first true believer and strongly
urged Obama to run. When Obama started to speak, Plouffe describes in *The Audacity To Win*, "he laid out why he was considering a run: the country needed deep, fundamental change;
Washington wasn't thinking long-term; and we had big challenges like energy and health care that had languished for decades; the special interests and lobbyists had too much power, and
the American people needed to once again trust and engage in
their democracy."

Then Obama's wife Michelle asked him directly, "What exactly do you think you can accomplish by getting the presidency?"
His response to her touched everyone in the room. It was as authentic and powerful a reply as hardened veterans like Hildebrand, Axelrod and Plouffe had ever heard . . .

On his way out, Plouffe told Axelrod candidly, "I was impressed by him. He clearly has a good sense of why he might want
to run, and it's not about power or politics or some long held am-
bition. I still think he doesn't do it [though]—how many people
have just sort of, last minute, with no planning, rolled the dice
and jumped into a presidential race against maybe the strongest
front-runner in history? With young kids to boot?"

But the slow drip of encouragement from all around him continued. Almost every public engagement Obama attended was

filled with growing, increasingly excited, and even expectant crowds. He couldn't shake it. In the meantime, one Senator after another secretly passed him signals that they would support him. Afraid as they were of offending Hillary Clinton, their likely future leader, they wanted Obama to know that they were looking for an alternative and, if he chose to run, more of them would support him than he might think. As John Heilemann and Mark Halperin report in *Game Change*, "Daschle, too, was on the case, and so was a coterie of Senators close to him, including Byron Dorgan and Kent Conrad, both of North Dakota. Ben Nelson of Nebraska, Bill Nelson of Florida, Barbara Boxer of California, and even Ted Kennedy—all were nudging Obama to take the plunge. Their conversations with Barack were surreptitious, a conspiracy of whispers. They told him that 2008 was going to be a change election and that he uniquely could embody transformation. They told him he might never get a better chance. They told him this could be his time."

His closest friend in the Senate was Dick Durbin, the senior Senator from Illinois. He told Obama candidly, "Sometimes in politics and leadership you can choose the time, but other times, the time chooses you"

Obama flew off to Hawaii for his winter vacation with family as he chewed over a final decision. Meanwhile, the chorus for an Obama candidacy was beginning to resonate closer and closer to home. Having traveled the turbulent road of several unsuccessful presidential campaigns in the past, Plouffe was agonizing over the possibility of entering another one. None of it fitted with his or his family's plans. He and his wife weighed the pros and cons, and then suddenly she lay down the gauntlet; but not in the way he expected.

He recounts what she said in his book: "'I have watched you struggle through campaign cycles for years now,' she told her husband. 'Your heart hasn't been in it since Gephardt took a pass in 2000. You tell me Barack Obama is authentic, one of the smartest people you have ever met, and in it for the right reasons. You say that you'll try to run a different campaign, getting people involved, especially young people and minorities. This seems like the kind of campaign you idealize. Sure, he probably won't win. But won't it be hypocritical if, after all the bemoaning of politics today, you don't answer the call here and try to do something about it?'"

"It took me aback." Says Plouffe. "She had plenty of valid reasons to oppose this step but now, to my surprise, she was challenging me to live up to my rhetoric. And what's more she was dead-on. This was a gut check. And if she thought we could potentially make it work with all the sacrifice it would entail for her and our son, it would be fraudulent of me not to address my cynicism by doing all I can to change it.

"She added, 'We'll have to figure out housing, pre-school and my work. I guess it would mean putting off grad school again. We just signed on to a new mortgage and we'll have to swing Chicago rent on top of it. It makes no sense for us right now. And frankly I'm not sure if a guy who was in the state senate three years ago has any business running for leader of the free world.

"'But we've been making a living working in and around politics for a long time, complaining all the while about how nasty it is. You believe in this guy. I believe in you. We can muster the courage to make this leap. I can figure out the finances, the logistics, and the family stuff. You just make sure we are part of a campaign that's worth it.'"

Plouffe telephoned Obama in Hawaii to let him know that, if he chose to run, he was in. Obama was as grateful as he was surprised.

On his return, Obama was still 50-50. According to Plouffe, "Obama was having a hard time making that final leap."

Then on the evening of January 6th 2007, late at night, Plouffe received a call from Obama. A call that is now seared into his memory forever. Obama uttered three words. "It's a go."

The campaign then started as chaotically and as unpredictably—with only a slim chance of victory—as it ended up being for virtually the entire first year. Indeed, Plouffe aptly portrayed this in his choice of title for the relevant chapter in *The Audacity To Win* "Taking Off While Affixing The Wings."

He describes the first months of frantic activity as they recruited a basic team and attempted to lay the groundwork for the campaign's official launch. "As we prepared for the announcement, the campaign still existed mostly on paper. We had no campaign office. No internal e-mail. No staff in the early states. No polling or policy work. We didn't yet have the ability to get campaign credit cards, so our staff out in the states and advance staff working on the announcement was forced to charge for everything on their personal cards and file for reimbursements. And Obama wanted to write much of the announcement speech himself. The odds of crashing were getting higher by the moment."

"Thus began a spring and summer of misery for the candidate." John Heilemann and Mark Halperin wrote in their account. "He'd been warned how hard this was going to be but he'd silently scoffed. And for the first few weeks it hadn't been hard at all—it had been a rush. But now the initial adrenaline surge was wearing off and Obama was facing the wretchedness of the reality he'd signed up for. It wasn't long before Axelrod and Plouffe wondered if he was nurturing second thoughts about his decision to run.

"The schedule was killing him. The fatigue was all consuming. The events piled up one on top of another making his temples ache . . . None of it would have been so bad if he had been per- forming up to his snuff. But he wasn't, and he knew it, and it pained him."

Hillary handled herself like a pro. She seemed to outshine him every time. In public forums where they would appear sequen- tially, the contrast was visible. Hillary was sharp and passionate, while Obama came across as rambling and vague. In short, he seemed like an amateur next to her. After one performance, re- viewing how things went in the plane on the way home, he prod- ded himself openly. "She was terrific," he told his team. "I was not."

Heilemann and Halperin noted that "Feelings of inadequacy had . . . never been a big part of the Obama psychic profile. But when it came to playing the role of a presidential candidate, he was experiencing them all the time."

But he plowed on, nevertheless. Even though it often looked like he could—even should—drop out, he stayed with it. And those closest to him knew why. It was in the answer he gave to Michelle, back in their first meeting of friends and advisors, when she asked him what difference he believed he could make by win- ning the presidency:

> "There are a lot of things I think I can accomplish, but two things I know. The first is, when I raise my hand and take that oath of office, there are millions of kids around this country who don't believe that it would ever be possible for them to be president of the United States. And for them the world would change on that day. And the second thing is, I think the world would look at us differently the day I got elected, because it would be a reaffirmation of what America is, about the constant perfecting of who we are."

The ups and downs continued, for the whole campaign, in fact. But it was this fundamental belief, together with a sincere policy vision of what he felt the country needed to get back on track, that kept him focused through the often grinding weeks and months ahead.

––––––

The understanding of concepts in psychology can sometimes be revolutionized by simple drawings. In 1908, two psychologists, Robert M. Yerkes and John Dillingham Dodson, after a series of experiments, drew a curve that transformed the way we understand the effects of tension and stress on human beings. Here is what is now known as the Yerkes-Dodson curve:

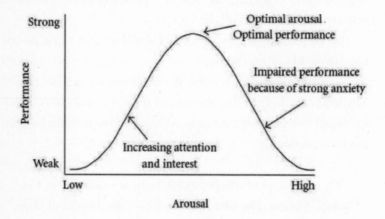

Basically, this graph shows us that as you increase your levels of arousal or tension in a given situation, your performance will also increase. But only up to a point. Beyond that point, higher levels of stress will mean that performance will start to decrease. The trick, then, is to always maintain an optimal level of arousal or tension in order to ensure an optimum performance.

What this curve also shows us is that we are able to achieve most in life at times when we are stretched. By opening ourselves up to the tension of life we allow ourselves to grow and, by allowing ourselves to grow, we will inevitably continue to achieve in one way or another. No one ever achieved anything in life by staying firmly rooted in their comfort zone.

The problem is, though, that we all have a natural resistance against any stress or tension at all. Our comfort zone, like a black hole, has a huge gravitational force that sucks us in, preventing us reaching out and traveling the road to personal growth and achievement. We tend to do this to ourselves when we are put off taking on something because it's too hard. We say, "no way, that's just too much of a stretch for me. I couldn't do that. I'd probably fail!" Maybe it's true, but in reality, whenever we do this we are actually asking ourselves the wrong question. The right question should always be "succeed or fail, win or lose, will taking this path be good for me?"

In other words, you should approach every challenge before you by discerning what you can gain from the journey itself, rather than to what destination it might lead you. The journey might be tough and, at times unpleasant, but is it one that will enable you and those around you to grow? Will it be for the betterment of yourself and others—regardless of the outcome? If so, then you have an obligation to proceed.

My writing of this book is an example of this. Writing it means taking a lot of time out of my schedule, energy, commitment and belief. And all the while I have no certainty as to whether or not anyone will buy it or any publishing deals will be forthcoming. It was something I contemplated for a long time before proceeding, until the right question came to me. Regardless of its commercial success or failure, would writing it be good for me? The answer was an unequivocal "yes." And this has been borne out by every moment I work on it. The very act of writing this book is enabling me to reflect and grow in myself too. Believe it or not, I actually find myself learning a lot from what I write. This is not uncommon. I remember reading Susan Jeffers' book, *Embracing Uncertainty* in which she spoke about how the book seemed to be writing itself and she found herself learning enormously from it. I am having the same experience too.

Don't get me wrong, I really do believe that this book will be a commercial success, but as I write I cannot be sure about how exactly it will pan out. However it does pan out, though, I will always be sure that it was the right thing to do.

So, don't avoid taking on a challenge just because the risk of failure seems too high. If it feels fundamentally right to you from the deepest parts of your self then take it on.

When Obama talked about "the constant perfecting of who we are," though he was talking about the country, whether he knew it or not, he was also referring to himself. The grueling race he was about to put himself through was also a means of constantly growing within. And for that reason, regardless of the outcome, he knew it was right for him to do. Early on, a journalist asked him how he would feel if he lost and, after a little thought, he said, "that would be right too." This was going to be a test of his character and, on that basis, he aimed to win it for himself as much as for anyone else.

———

Like Obama, Hillary Clinton had a keen interest in Indian culture. In fact, during one trip to India she jokingly told a local official that her interest in the country was such that she ought to be known as the Senator for Punjab. In the early days of the primary campaign, the Obama team picked up on this. A research document entitled "Hillary Clinton, D-Punjab," was produced, ridiculing her for the comment, and found its way to the press.

The story appeared in *The New York Times* and, as soon as he read it, a furious Obama was on the phone to David Plouffe. "This is the first time I am embarrassed by my campaign." He told him. "I never want this to happen again . . . I want controls in place and I want you to take personal responsibility for it. I don't care what the other campaigns are doing. We can't use that as a standard. Get control of it or I won't allow us to send anything but our schedule out to the press."

Plouffe instantly acknowledged the mistake. "We had screwed up, and in a way that could be uniquely damaging. For other campaigns this would be a blip on the radar. But we had promised a different standard, and this was about as far as possible from the type of campaign we had pledged to run."

They had all learned something in that moment; Obama was as serious about the way they ran their campaign as the result it achieved. From that point forth, the rest of the team was fully signed up to the strategy too; this was going to be an endeavor in which the means would be equally as important as the ends.

––––––

So the right course is about growing, regardless of the achievement itself. It is fine to have goals, but the primary goal should always be growth. Whatever course you chart should first and foremost be about the ongoing challenge of determining who you are, and of discerning and manifesting your values. Ultimate objectives or end points should be held lightly and subject to change and adjustment where necessary. What should be the constant is the means; the way you go about doing what you do. That is why my own favored school of psychotherapy, Acceptance and Commitment Therapy (ACT), emphasizes the importance of values. In introducing the subject in his book *Get Out Of Your Mind And Into Your Life*, Steven Hayes starts with a small list of what values are not:

> *Values are not goals*
> *Values are not feelings*
> *Values are not outcomes*
> *Values do not mean our paths are always straight*
> *Values are not in the future*

Values are likened more to a direction of travel, rather than the destination. It's like saying, "I want to go east." There is no point at which you will reach "east," so it's more about which way you travel than where you end up. Translating this into psychological terms usually means locating adjectives that you would like to attach to yourself or adverbs to actions you believe to be important, e.g. to be an attentive parent, to be a dependable employee, to be a loving husband.

In ACT we sometimes talk about 10 key domains for values that most people have. Here's an excellent exercise that will help you locate your values in each of these domains.

LIFE VALUES EXERCISE

Let's explore the ten key value domains and put together a values statement for you. First of all, start by writing a sentence or two—on a separate piece of paper—in response to each of these questions below, which relate to each of the main value domains:

1. **Marriage/Couple/Intimate Relationships.** What kind of person would you most like to be, in the context of an intimate relationship?

2. **Parenting.** This domain is not just for parents but also for anyone who spends time with and takes responsibility for children in their lives; perhaps as an uncle, aunt, godparent, teacher, coach, and neighbor. What kind of person would you like to be in the context of this role?

3. **Other Family Relations.** Think of your other family relations. What kind of a cousin, daughter, grandparent, or in-law would you like to be?

4. **Friendships/Social Relations.** What kind of a friend would you like to be?

5. **Career/Employment.** What kind of an employee or boss would you like to be? What would you like to stand for in your work?

6. **Education/Training/Personal Development.** There are many forms of learning we all engage in throughout our life. How would you like to engage in this area of your life and what kind of a learner do you want to be?

7. **Recreation/Leisure.** Leisure and recreation is important to all of us. Think about your interests and hobbies and work out what kind of an enthusiast/fan/follower/player/traveler etc. you would like to be.

8. **Spirituality.** This is meant in the broader sense and may or may not include organized religion. What kind of a person do you see yourself as being in this respect?

9. **Citizenship.** Think about how you contribute to society and the wider community. You might best be able

to locate this in terms of your local area, your country, your areas of interest and passion, the company you work for or several other dimensions. What kind of a person would you like to be in this aspect of your life?

10. **Health/Physical Well-Being.** What kind of a person would you like to see yourself as in relation to this?

Now, some of these values will be more important and meaningful to you than others. That's fine. The next task, then, is to rank these different values in order of importance to you. Once you have done that, take a look at the figure below. Now, within the body of the outline person on the next page, list the top 5 or 6 sentences you have written on the paper in order of importance to you . . .

LIFE VALUES STATEMENT

This is your life values statement. Put your name at the top. If you want, you can download it from http://www.obamakarma .org/values.html, fill it out and carry it in your wallet, just so you can glance at it—like the North Star—whenever you need direction.

Any goals you choose in life should be consistent with these values. Not only this, but your goals should actually enhance these values and, in many ways, serve as a testing ground for them. They should stretch you and enable you to more deeply fulfill them in the process. As long as this remains more important to you than any goal itself, you'll never go far wrong.

Running for president certainly served this purpose for Obama. But that was as of nothing compared to the trial of the presidency itself.

Challenging himself and challenging those around him has always been Obama's style. "We do big things" is his consistent theme, and this applies as much to his presidency as it did to his unorthodox and audacious campaign for president. It is for this reason that reforming healthcare—a goal attempted and failed by previous administrations for over half a century—became a key aim for him on reaching the Oval Office.

At the time of Obama's inauguration, over thirty million Americans were not covered by any health insurance at all; a unique scenario in the developed world, with virtually every other industrialized nation enjoying universal coverage. In addition, hundreds of thousands of those who had been paying for health insurance for the entirety of their lives suddenly discovered, when they made a claim, that their insurance would not cover them due to a supposed "pre-existing condition" which the insurance company insisted must have been in place and voided the insurance. Thousands of sick Americans were going bankrupt as a result, often losing their homes and even ultimately their lives, in a fight to keep up with their ever-escalating medical bills.

From day one in his transition office in Chicago, a couple of months before assuming the presidency, Obama began to plan out his strategy for healthcare and put together structures and teams that would facilitate the passage of a comprehensive bill into law.

"I'd rather be here for four years and get something done," he would tell senior advisors, "than walk around those halls for eight years and get nothing done."

Obama's determination on the issue, in the face of early resistance, even from within, is well documented by Richard Wolffe in *Revival*.

"There were few around him who thought health care was the right way for Obama to define his first year. David Axelrod was more interested in a big education bill. Several Senators pushed for action on climate change. But Obama stuck to health care. It was what he worked on in the Illinois State Senate; what he ran on to get elected to the United States Senate; what he talked about almost every rally on the Presidential campaign trail. 'This is a huge issue for him and something he felt was going to be a personal measure of his success as President,' said one senior aide. 'And it is something the First Lady also feels very strongly about. African-American leaders feel he ignores their issues, but the health disparities in this country are felt most horribly in their community. I've always felt you can't overlook that piece of it. He spent a lot of time on the South Side of Chicago with laid off steel workers.'"

From the outset, however, the legislation began to run into difficulties. As it made its tortuous path through Congress a fervently antagonistic narrative began to emerge, like an escalating drum beat, out of cable TV. Its energy started to percolate into the public sphere. Fox News began actively coordinating demonstrations against it; these demonstrations, known as "tea parties," soon began taking on a life of their own. With an increasingly elaborate organization behind opposition to the bill came a deafening noise level that ultimately became the focus of all media coverage around it. The sight of one Democratic lawmaker after another being heckled and shouted down in town hall meetings started to become a regular event. Words like "government takeover of health care" and notions such as "a bureaucrat sitting between you and your doctor" began to grip the public consciousness.

The essence of the plan, however, was simple; if every American was mandated to purchase health insurance then insurance companies—in receipt of those millions of new customers (most of whom wouldn't be ill)—could afford to drop their premiums substantially, making it affordable to all, and also cease the practice of denying coverage based on pre-existing conditions. The new legislation would also ensure insurance costs were kept low by establishing state based market places, or "exchanges" where people could go to compare prices, requiring companies to compete and keep their premiums low. And for people who could not afford it at all, e.g. the unemployed, they would be entitled to a subsidized plan, similar to the plan enjoyed by federal employees including Congressmen and Senators.

This, in fact, was almost exactly the same system implemented by Mitt Romney in Massachusetts when he was governor there, and it was the same plan advocated by the Republican Party in the Clinton years as an alternative to his plans. That didn't prevent its mischaracterization, however, in many quarters, as an attempted socialist redrawing of America.

Nevertheless, as the single biggest manifestation of his values—and major reason for seeking the presidency in the first place—Obama continued to push lawmakers to make progress. And at the same time he continued to attempt to counter the malicious narrative that was taking hold with the public. He organized an especially dedicated speech to both houses of Congress to calm nerves:

> "I am not the first President to take up this cause, but I am determined to be the last. It has now been nearly a century since Theodore Roosevelt first called for health care reform. And ever since, nearly every President and Congress, whether Democrat or Republican, has attempted to meet this challenge in some way . . .
>
> "We are the only advanced democracy on Earth—the only wealthy nation—that allows such hardships for millions of its people. There are now more than thirty million American citizens who cannot get coverage. In just a two-year period, one in every three Americans goes without health care coverage at some point. And every day, 14,000 Americans lose their coverage. In other words, it can happen to anyone.
>
> "But the problem that plagues the health care system is not just a problem of the uninsured. Those who do have insurance have never had less security and stability than they do today. More and more Americans worry that if you move, lose your job, or change your job, you'll lose your health insurance too. More and more Americans pay their premiums, only to discover that their insurance company has dropped their coverage when they get sick, or won't pay the full cost of care. It happens every day.
>
> "One man from Illinois lost his coverage in the middle of chemotherapy because his insurer found that he hadn't reported gallstones that he didn't even know about. They delayed his treatment, and he died because of it. Another

woman from Texas was about to get a double mastectomy when her insurance company canceled her policy because she forgot to declare a case of acne. By the time she had her insurance reinstated, her breast cancer more than doubled in size. That is heartbreaking, it is wrong, and no one should be treated that way in the United States of America . . .

"I understand how difficult this health care debate has been. I know that many in this country are deeply skeptical that government is looking out for them. I understand that the politically safe move would be to kick the can further down the road—to defer reform one more year, or one more election, or one more term.

"But that's not what the moment calls for. That's not what we came here to do. We did not come to fear the future. We came here to shape it. I still believe we can act even when it's hard. I still believe we can replace acrimony with civility, and gridlock with progress. I still believe we can do great things, and that here and now we will meet history's test.

"Because that is who we are. That is our calling. That is our character."

With the basic architecture laid out, the House of Representatives passed a first draft of the bill in a historic vote. And slowly but surely, through a series of interlocking negotiations and after several months of back and forth, the Senate passed its own version too.

At this point, Obama stepped up a gear and started working intensely with both bodies to coalesce the legislation into a single bill that could make final passage through both chambers of Congress—a process known as reconciliation. This is the last stage in lawmaking, before a bill is passed to the president to sign.

He brought key players over to the West Wing and juggled numerous meetings between rooms, forging compromises and edging the two bills together, inch-by-inch, towards a final settlement.

All the while, however, across the skies, a political missile was hurtling its way towards the White House. Unbeknownst to any of the senior figures toiling away on the healthcare bill, all of their work was about to be blown away by a projectile from Massachusetts.

It was easily the safest liberal state in the union and that's why, after mourning the sad passing of Senator Ted Kennedy, no one gave a second thought to the special election to replace him in the Senate. Not even, it seemed, the Democratic Party candidate, Martha Coakley, who promptly went for a prolonged vacation in the middle of her election campaign.

By the time the possibility of her defeat registered on the White House radar, they were already at the point of no return. In *Revival*, Richard Wolffe reports: "Inside the White House, there was what one senior official called 'total meltdown' as they realized it was already too late to intervene. 'How could we miss this?' asked one incredulous campaign veteran. 'Some of us were hearing what was going on and asking what was happening. The answer was nothing. The political shop wasn't doing anything. The DNC [Democratic National Committee] was doing nothing. They only had one race to look after.'"

The consequences of this were dire. They previously had just enough votes to pass a final merged bill in the Senate, and now that was about to evaporate. Wolffe describes the mood in the White House: "The sickening sensation of imminent defeat. The sense of waste and frustration after months of long days, short nights, conference calls and back-to-back meetings."

In the end Coakley was soundly beaten by the Republican candidate Scott Brown, irrevocably changing the balance of power in the Senate. They now had no way of passing the reconciled bill and all work on it came to an abrupt halt.

The weeks that followed saw a West Wing that looked like it had been hit by a bomb. Staffers walked around like the living dead. Even Obama, the man from whom they all took their cue, seemed uncertain what to do next. Was this it? Would his attempt at solving the nation's healthcare problem end in the same way as it had for every Democratic president before him? The media had universally proclaimed this to be the case. Even lawmakers from his own party were pontificating in the same vein, both in private and in public. Obama's ever-combative Chief of Staff Rahm Emanuel, in a bid to try and rescue some skeletal victory, suggested narrowing the bill down to a few uncontroversial tweaks so at least they could claim an achievement of some sort, but this wasn't Obama's style, as he told ABC's George Stephanopoulos, "I could have said, 'well, we'll just do what's safe. We'll just take on those things that are completely non-controversial.' The problem is the things that are non-controversial end up being the things that don't solve the problem. And this is true on every issue."

An idea started to surface that perhaps the Senate didn't need to pass another version of the bill. If the House of Representatives agreed to pass the same legislation that had gone through the Senate then it would still work. Obama invited the House Speaker Nancy Pelosi to the Oval Office with Senate Majority Leader, Harry Reid to try and see if they could sketch something through.

"Why don't you pass the Senate bill?" Reid fired off to Pelosi at the start of the gathering. "I can't do it because I don't have the votes," Pelosi shot back. "And don't you ever say the House has to pass the Senate bill," she warned. "I need time. I have to bring people along. People have to get over the shock. They have to see what the consequences are if we fail. If you people tell everyone to pass the Senate bill, I won't have any room to maneuver."

A plan started to take shape, however. If the Senate made commitments to pass amendments to the bill after it had already passed the House and become law, that might convince some House members into voting for the originally worded Senate bill. A pathway was before them, but what Obama needed to do now was trust. The legislators in the House needed time. They had to consider their options and find their own way to the solution. No one could force it upon them. So Obama decided to give them the space and respect they needed.

Many people took this to mean the opposite of what it was; that Obama was no longer as committed to healthcare reform as he once was. Even his State of the Union speech in March spent relatively little time on the issue. All the time, however, he was patiently watching and waiting. His core value of mirroring the respect he is given by others back to them was being tested like never before.

Others around him started to agitate about what Congress was doing and whether or not they would come round to passing the Senate version of the bill, but Obama continually provided reassurance. "Relax, they will come to understand that they can't walk away."

Finally, Pelosi called a vote in the House. On the eve of the vote, Obama went up to Capitol Hill and delivered a last minute pep talk to the Democratic lawmakers about to cast arguably the most important vote of their lives. It was a short speech, but a profound one, nevertheless, that moved many. It was not about winning, scoring points or ticking off goals, but about doing what's right, regardless of whether or not it is ultimately followed by success or failure. The only goal he asked them to pursue was the goal of being true to themselves and their values, and staying in what ever tension it took to see it through.

"Every once in a while, every once in a while a moment comes where you have the chance to vindicate all those best hopes you had about yourself, about this country, where you have a chance to make good on those promises that you made in all those town meetings and all those constituency breakfasts and all that traveling through the district, all those people who looked you in the eye and you said, 'You know what? You're right. The system isn't working for you and I'm going to make it a little bit better.' And this is one of those moments. This is one of those times. We are not bound to win, but we are bound to be true. We are not bound to succeed but we are bound to let whatever light we have shine."

Wolffe describes the scene in the White House the next day as they huddled together to watch the vote in Congress. "They gathered in the Roosevelt Room to watch the voting even later than they anticipated. They were assured the votes were there, but after Massachusetts—after all the false starts and misplaced hopes over the last year—they were holding their breath as the numbers of the screen edged upwards to 219, three more than they needed . . . Inside the House chamber, the Democrats started chanting 'Yes we can!' Inside the West Wing, Obama's staff cheered and applauded as the president walked in and high-fived Emanuel."

After a press statement, Obama suggested a staff party on the Truman Balcony. He took off his tie and felt the tension that had built up around him over the last eighteen months, like deep ocean water pressure around a descending submarine, start to finally ease. He had been tested, pushed and derailed more than once but he had remained true to himself throughout, and in the process, achieved his—and his entire party's—most cherished goal. Now was the time to celebrate with the whole team who made it possible.

"I don't want to ruin a good party with a big speech," he told them at the start of the gathering. "We've had tough times but we've done something big. We just accomplished what we all came here to do."

It was a warm night. Beer bottles clinked and smiles twinkled everywhere.

"I am so happy," he told Valerie Jarrett. "It feels far better than election night."

"Why?" She asked him.

"Because election night was just a means to get to this night. That was not nearly the cause to celebrate as actually accomplishing something."

———

Our values are like the orientation of our sails as we chart our course through life and the different places we visit along the way. There is never a final destination or goal. They keep changing and we keep moving, and the realization of this is what will help us shift our focus a little from the destinations themselves, toward the way we conduct the journey. To extend the metaphor further, the wind in our sales is our pain. As discussed in previous chapters, we all contain a well of energy within us that is based on the pain we will inevitably accumulate through life. This pain then acts as the fuel that drives us forward. It could drive us forward in destructive ways or, with a little bit of channeling and attention, drive us forward in very productive ways instead. That's where our values come in. In the same way the sails channel the wind to enable us to journey forth, so our values effectively channel our pain to facilitate our growth.

The first task, of course, is always awareness. No sailor could ever harness the power of the wind into his sails without first gaining an awareness of the wind itself—its quality and how it moves. That is our first task as sailors of life when it comes to our own pain. We should open ourselves up to an awareness of our pain and not shrink or hide from it. This requires, what Pema Chödrön refers to as a "warrior quality." It means fearlessness in the face of life; a determination to face whatever may come our way. Chödrön talks about how she relearns this lesson every year from the ravens that fly outside the abbey where she teaches by the mountains of windy Nova Scotia.

"The wilder the weather is, the more the ravens love it. They have the time of their lives in the winter, when the wind gets much stronger and there's lots of ice and snow. They challenge the wind. They get up on the tops of the trees and they hold on with their claws and then they grab on with their beaks as well. At some point they just let go into the wind and let it blow them away. Then they play on it, they float on it. After a while they'll go back to the tree and start over. It's a game. Once I saw them in an incredible hurricane-velocity wind, grabbing each other's feet and dropping and then letting go and flying out. It was like a circus act. The animals and plants here are hardy and fearless and playful and joyful; the elements have strengthened them. In order to exist here they have had to develop a zest for challenge and for life. As you can see, it adds up to tremendous beauty and inspiration and uplifted feeling. The same goes for us."

So be like a raven in the wind as you face the challenges life brings to you. Know that along the way there will be pain, obstacles, failures and set backs, but because it is right for you, you're going to do it anyway. And remember that each obstacle and setback is of value too.

In another of her books, *The Places That Scare You*, Chödrön writes about the importance of seeing obstacles as teachers:

> "If there is no teacher around to give us direct personal guidance on how to stop causing harm, never fear! Life itself will provide opportunities for learning how to hold our seat. Without the inconsiderate neighbor, where will we find the chance to practice patience? Without the office bully how could we ever get the chance to know the energy of anger so intimately that it looses its destructive power?"

By allowing yourself to face the pain that challenges you, you will realize that, rather than being destroyed by it, you are in fact transforming yourself into a form of pain processing plant. The more you face it, the more efficient you will become.

Sometimes you will get it wrong and shrink back into your comfort zone, but that's OK too. All progress comes in waves. Just like the waves on a shoreline that appear to be flowing back and forth when, in fact, the tide is gradually working its way in one direction—in or out—the whole time, so it is with progress on anything substantial and meaningful in life; two steps forward and one step back. Remember, dealing with the pain of failure is also a stepping-stone on the road to success. Visualizing the way in which our pain generates energy in the form of thoughts, feelings, motivations and drives within us will help us to know it better and so equip us to channel it. The next meditation is designed to help us with that.

ALKA-SELTZER MEDITATION

Read these notes then close your eyes and take yourself gently through each step. Alternatively, you will find this guided meditation, for you to simultaneously listen to and practice, online at www.obamakarma.org/alka.html:

- Sit or stand in a comfortable position. Keep your back straight and unsupported, so you're relaxed but upright.
- Start by taking a few deep breaths and feel your lungs fill with clean air on the in-breath, and empty completely on the out-breath.
- Gently close your eyes or, if you prefer, leave them open but focused only softly on what is before you.
- Now spend a moment listening to the sounds around you, around the room and outside it. The sound of stillness, motion, noise or what ever happens to be there.

- Start to feel inside your own body; the bands of light and dark, pleasure and pain, heaviness and lightness that are contained within you.
- Now, begin to focus your awareness on the areas of emotional pain within you. Parts of you that feel heavier and sadder than others. They represent the accumulation of stress, disappointment, anxieties and difficulties from the past and present.
- Now, using metaphor, consider the pain as if it were a tablet. An Alka-Seltzer fizzing away deep inside you. As it does, it produces bubbles that travel through your mind and body. These bubbles are all the thoughts and feelings that you have inside you.

- You are the glass containing the tablet and the fizz of bubbles flowing off it.
- You are not the tablet—the pain—and you are not the bubbles—your thoughts and feelings that flow from it—but you contain them all.
- Sit in stillness for a few moments observing your inner Alka-Seltzer fizzing away producing all the different thoughts and feelings that travel through your mind.
- Just hold it and watch it all for a few minutes. This is the ultimate reality of your inner world. It is not good or bad. It is what is. Observe it without judgment.

- After several minutes, gradually return to the broader awareness of the room around you; imagine its features before opening your eyes, looking around and giving yourself a few moments to reorient.

Try this whenever you can. Simply close your eyes, take a few deep breaths and sit with the Alka-Seltzer within.

HOMEWORK

Despite the title, this book and self-improvement course has actually been about one person all along: not Barack Obama, but you. Obama has been a good example of someone who has learned a fundamental lesson of life, and that is that the most important and powerful source of wisdom for each of us is that within ourselves.

Each of the lessons focuses on different ways in which you can tap into and harness the wisdom within you:

The first lesson was about locating the rigidity that is part of our make-up as humans. By working with it, rather than running away from or denying it, we can then unlock the power of flexibility that helps us achieve our goals more effectively by flowing with the currents around us, rather than fighting against them.

The second lesson was about communing with and relaxing into the well of uncertainty that sits within each one of us.

The third lesson was about embracing the imperfect world—both inside and out—and making true acceptance our starting point in any endeavor; for it is the only starting point from which we can ever achieve effective change.

Lesson four focused on the shadow. It is a part of each of us that we often deny; yet the very act of recognition and bringing light to it can dramatically transform and improve the course of our life journey.

Lesson five took us to a level deeper to connect with the compassion—the heart—that lies at the core of each of us.

Lesson six showed how a respect for yourself can only ever lead to an equal out flowing of the same, bringing out the best, not only in yourself, but of all those around you too.

In lesson seven we started to take a closer look at our pain and how changing our perception of it from something to be avoided to the opposite—something to nurture, give space to and spend time with—will transform it into a truly powerful force for inner growth.

And finally, in lesson eight, we looked at how to keep living a life that always challenges us to stay in touch with all these aspects of ourselves and so keep growing, shining and progressing all the time.

These are the ingredients to our success—to our lifelong expansion and continued liberation—and they lie, not in the outside world, but within each and every one of us. It's just a question of getting in touch. And as we do this by reaching deeper into ourselves, we will find that we are able to reach further out as well.

The further out we reach, the more we will be able to see just how like everyone else we all are; just how changeable we all are, just how full of worries and anxieties we all are, and just how hung up we all are on how people see us and what the world makes of us. Realizing that we're not so different from everybody else ultimately helps us forgive ourselves for not being perfect, and forgive others for their imperfections too.

In other words, the deeper the bond we develop with ourselves, the deeper the bond we are able to develop with the rest of humanity too.

And as we do, we will become increasingly able to view the world from the perspective of our observer self. Our still, non-judgmental, uninvolved, unaffected, observer self. This is a function we all possess, the deepest function of all. It is the part of us that does not exist in time or space. It is not inside us or outside us either—it is nothing that we can put a finger on, locate or describe. But it is the part of us that sees every other part of us and everything else before us as well. It is the part of us that we contact when we are meditating or being mindful, i.e. just watching what we do—without labeling, thinking or judging. It's here with you right now as you read this book.

Notice yourself reading these words on the page before you.

You are not just the reader; you can also observe yourself—the reader—reading.

This is your observer self.

Or perhaps we should call it your nothing self, as it is the point from which you observe everything (including your physical self), and so contains nothing itself. You can contact it, just as you did now, anytime you wish. Doing so will vastly deepen your experience of life. It will differ profoundly from your normal physical experience.

Here's a summary of what I mean; comparing the characteristics and experience of your physical self to your observer/nothing self:

Your physical self . . .	Your observer self . . .
hopes and fears	watches and wonders
is doing and striving	is being and standing
is time based	is timeless
is goal driven	is goalless
exists in physical and material form	has no form and exists in void

Most of the meditations in this book have been about trying to help you find this place. It is not a place to which your thoughts or feelings are attached, but it is a place from which it can all be viewed without judgment or reaction. If you believe in God or religion, you may be able to link some of those concepts to this place, but there is no need to do so if you do not. It is what it is.

The more you meditate, the more you will contact this deepest aspect of yourself. It is like training a muscle. The more you exercise the stronger you become. So that is your homework at the end of this program: Whether through the meditations and exercises described here, or other forms of meditation or mindfulness, try to use every opportunity you can to tune in to your observer, nothing self.

A useful way to access it, in my experience, is when you are engaged in activities that do not require much conscious thought, like doing the dishes or taking a shower. Just step back in your mind for a moment and watch yourself doing what you're doing. It sometimes helps to label what you observe, like "cleaning" or "walking," and when your cooling fan minds starts to take you away from the moment, watch that too and say "thinking."

Practicing this kind of presence means you fear life less and embrace it more. As you do, you will be building a resilience that helps you face life whatever it brings.

Despite this, however, sometimes you will fail. Sometimes you will get it wrong. Sometimes the waves of life will overwhelm you. But then you will stand up. And the next time you will find it easier to stand up again. And each time you do, you will be able to keep walking—and do so in the direction of your choosing.

And that is the only Karma that truly counts.

ACKNOWLEDGMENTS

Though writing can be a lonely business, no writer is ever an island. There are always bridges to the outside world that help shape and test the project as it grows. On this occasion I have been blessed with several people who have brought their diverse array of experiences to bear and shone a torch on the ideas I have been working on. Their editing, critiques, suggestions and strategies have been invaluable to me and that is why I have been looking forward to the part of the book where I get to thank them.

The first two are mother and daughter: Doreen Montgomery is my agent. Together with her professional partner and daughter Caroline, they both helped me in my initial brainstorming, planning and strategy for the book. Doreen has been a stalwart in support of my work from the beginning, and this book was no exception.

Jarmila Gorman was both my editor and early stage one woman focus group. She was as close to the target audience as it is probably possible to be and, together with her own experience in self-help writing and editing, she became an excellent sounding board and constructive critic. Later stage copy editing was completed by James Houston and, though we never communicated directly, the high standard of his work and the constructive perfectionism with which he evidently approaches it, spoke for itself and easily warrants a heartfelt thank you.

Finally, and most importantly, my publishing and PR partners at February Books, Gretchen Crary and Dee Dee DeBartlo; they got the project from day one—its value and its potential—and the moment they came on board, they applied themselves to it with a tireless energy that has sometimes left even me breathless. Their passionate professionalism, experience and contacts have served as the launch pad for this book and I will always be grateful for the opportunity to work with them and for what, no doubt, they will do for this project.

SOURCE NOTES

LESSON 1: SIT WITH UNCERTAINTY

1. White House transcript; Remarks by the President at a Memorial Service for the Victims of the Shooting in Tucson, Arizona, January 12th, 2011.
2. White House transcript; remarks by the President in commencement address at the university of Notre Dame, May 17th, 2009.
3. Nick Robinson, *Too Late?*, bbc.co.uk, March 16th 2011.
4. Nick Robinson, *Cameron's First War*, bbc.co.uk, March 17th 2011.
5. Mark Mardell, *World Await Obama Libya Decision*, bbc.co.uk, March 16th 2011.
6. Rachel Maddow, *Obama tries to change "war President" narrative*, msnbc.com, The Rachel Maddow Show, March 21st 2011.
7. White House transcript; remarks by the President in Address to the Nation on Libya, National Defense University, March 28th, 2011.
8. Christina Patterson, "Why, In Spite Of Everything, I Still Love Obama," *Huffington Post*, March 26th, 2011.
9. Tom Malinowski, "The Timeless Paradox," *The New Republic*, March 27th 2011.

LESSON 2: BE FLEXIBLE LIKE WATER

1. David Plouffe, *The Audacity To Win; The Inside Story and Lessons of Barack Obama's Historic Victory* (Viking, 2009: pp. 199–203).

2. Barack Obama, *Dreams From My Father* (Canongate, 2007; pp. 67–68, 212–221).

3. Toby Harnden, "Barack Obama Declares 'The War On Terror' Is Over," *The Telegraph*, May 27th 2010.

4. Elisabeth Bumiller, Charlie Savage, Steven Lee Myers, Adam Ellick, Ismail Khan, "Behind The Hunt For Bin Laden," *The New York Times*, May 2nd 2011.

5. Mark Mazzetti & Scott Shane, "Data Show Bin Laden Plots; CIA Hid Near Raid House," *The New York Times*, May 5th 2011.

6. Giles Whittell & Michael Evans, "US Races To Unravel Bin Laden's Secrets," *The Times,* May 13th 2011.

LESSON 3: EMBRACE IMPERFECTION

1. Richard Wolffe, *Revival, The Struggle For Survival In The Obama White House* (Crown, 2010: pp. 37–38).

2. Steven Erlanger, "Surprise Nobel For Obama Stirs Praise And Doubts," *New York Times*, October 9, 2009.

3. White House transcript; Remarks by the President at the Acceptance of the Nobel Peace Prize, December 10, 2009.

4. Richard Wolffe, *Renegade, The Making of a President* (Crown, 2009: pp. 176–178).

5. Mark Heilemann & Mark Halperin, *Game Change, Obama and the Clintons, McCain and Palin, and the Race of a Lifetime* (Harper, 2010: pp. 237–238).

6. David Plouffe, *The Audacity To Win; The Inside Story and Lessons of Barack Obama's Historic Victory* (Viking, 2009: pp. 207–213).

7. White House transcript; The President's Speech in Cairo: A New Beginning, June 4th, 2009.

LESSON 4: MAKE SPACE FOR SHADOWS

1. Richard Wolffe, *Revival, The Struggle for Survival in the Obama White House* (Crown, 2010: pp. 116).

2. Chris Frates, "Closed-door Health Care Reform Decried," *Politico*, October 27, 2009.

3. Pema Chodron, *The Wisdom of No Escape: How to love yourself and your world* (Element, 2004: pp. 15–17).

LESSON 5: CONNECT TO YOUR CORE

1. Pema Chodron, *The Wisdom of No Escape: How to love yourself and your world* (Element, 2004: pp. 2–8).

2. Richard Wolffe, *Revival, The Struggle for Survival in the Obama White House* (Crown, 2010: pp. 64–65).

3. White House transcript; Remarks By The President On Fiscal Policy, April 13th, 2011.

4. Eugene Robinson, "Lines In The Sand," Washington Post, April 15th, 2011.

LESSON 6: MIRROR RESPECT

1. Richard Wolffe, *Renegade, The Making of a President* (Crown, 2009: pp. 71–103, 315).

2. Mark Heilemann & Mark Halperin, *Game Change, Obama and the Clintons, McCain and Palin, and the Race of a Lifetime* (Harper, 2010: pp. 430–436).

3. Joe Klein, "Obama's Team Of Rivals," Time Magazine, June 18th, 2008.

4. Richard Wolffe, *Revival, The Struggle for Survival in the Obama White House* (Crown, 2010: pp. 249–251).

LESSON 7: GAIN STRENGTH FROM PAIN

1. Don Gonyea "Obama's Loss May Have Aided White House Bid," NPR, September 19th, 2007.

2. Christopher Wills, "Obama learned from failed Congress run," *USA Today*, October 24th, 2007

3. Steve Hayes and Spencer Smith, *Get Out of Your Mind and Into Your Life* (New Harbinger, 2005: p. 130).

4. David Plouffe, *The Audacity To Win; The Inside Story and Lessons of Barack Obama's Historic Victory* (Viking, 2009: pp. 138–153).

5. Richard Wolffe, *Renegade, The Making of a President* (Crown, 2009: pp. 114–116).

6. Barack Obama, *Dreams From My Father* (Canongate, 2007; pp. 70–71, 75-76, 104, 427–430).

LESSON 8: STAY IN THE TENSION

1. David Plouffe, *The Audacity To Win; The Inside Story and Lessons of Barack Obama's Historic Victory* (Viking, 2009: pp. 11, 25–26, 28–31, 73).

2. Richard Wolffe, *Renegade, The Making of a President* (Crown, 2009: pp. 52–53).

3. Mark Heilemann & Mark Halperin, *Game Change, Obama and the Clintons, McCain and Palin, and the Race of a Lifetime* (Harper, 2010: pp. 33–37, 107–109).

4. Steve Hayes and Spencer Smith, *Get Out of Your Mind and Into Your Life* (New Harbinger, 2005: p. 155–176).

5. Richard Wolffe, *Revival, The Struggle for Survival in the Obama White House* (Crown, 2010: pp. 51–53, 145–150).

6. Pema Chodron, *The Wisdom of No Escape: How to love yourself and your world* (Element, 2004: p. 88).

7. Pema Chodron, *The Places That Scare You* (Element, 2001: p. 174).